What Does God Do from 9 to 5?

Ronald R. Johnson

Author of *Customer Service and the Imitation of Christ*

ISBN: 1505869641
ISBN-13: 9781505869644

DEDICATION

Just after I graduated from college, I traveled America's Pacific Northwest sharing stories about how I had found God in daily secular life. I told my listeners that what I had experienced in school settings, they could discover in their places of employment.

Audiences in a number of congregations paid me the supreme compliment of challenging me. "Is it true?" they asked. "Can we really find God in the workplace?" They posed earnest, detailed questions that I couldn't answer, because I lacked both work experience and theological depth. But those people became my people, and for over thirty years I've sought answers on their behalf.

This volume is dedicated to them.

CONTENTS

ACKNOWLEDGMENTS

The cover was designed by Melissa Houtz, with photography by Emily Johnson.

Unless otherwise noted, the Scripture quotations contained herein are from the New Revised Standard Version Bible, copyright © 1989 by the Division of Christian Education of the National Council of Churches of Christ in the U.S.A., and are used by permission. All rights reserved.

References to Clifford® the Big Red Dog are from Norman Bridwell, *Clifford's Best Friend: A Story about Emily Elizabeth* (New York: Scholastic, 2000).

The discussion about the history of the PET Milk Company is drawn from Martin L. Bell, *A Portrait of Progress: A Business History of Pet Milk Company from 1885 to 1960* (St Louis: Pet Milk Company, 1962).

My wife Nancy and daughter Emily have been a constant source of encouragement, as have Senior Pastor Barry T. Petrucci and the members of Portage Chapel Hill United Methodist Church in Portage, Michigan (USA). Our congregation's bibliographical wonder, Kathy Willhite, was the inspiration for the character NB, in spirit but not in appearance.

1 SIMON SAYS

"The trouble with you Christians is—"

I'm reading the news online and my best friend, Savannah, pokes me with her elbow. "Dayton, listen to this!"

All around the bus, heads turn.

It's Simon, the British guy who shares trenchant observations of American life during our morning bus ride downtown. He usually sits in one of the front seats that face inward toward the aisle so that everybody can see and hear him. He's always provocative, but it's unlike him to start a religious argument. Glancing in his direction, I realize what has happened: Sammy the Soul Saver strikes again.

Sammy has a heart for evangelism. I respect him for that. He fearlessly sits beside commuters and asks them if they know the Lord. The problem is, he focuses entirely on death. It's all about snatching souls from the fires of hell. If you say the magic words, you're set for eternity. He says nothing about spiritual growth. It's all a legal transaction for him, and it's over in a jiffy if you cooperate.

But Simon is not the cooperative sort.

"The trouble with you Christians," he says, "is that you don't see the relevance of Christianity to your own lives, so you don't know how to get a religious conversation started." He stares at Sammy and waits for comprehension. It's a long wait.

Sammy shakes his head. "I don't—I, uh—"

"Casual conversations don't furnish you with opportunities, because God doesn't have anything to do with real life. So you change the subject. You don't know how to carry on a proper conversation about your religion."

"Well, excuse me for not following etiquette," says Sammy.

"Breaches in etiquette I can tolerate, but there's a larger point at issue here. You want to witness to people about your faith? Fine! But you're unable to do it from the subject at hand, and that fact should trouble you, because it means that your faith has no bearing on the things that people are already thinking and talking about. Look, if you can't tell me about God without changing the subject, then God must not have any meaningful connection to my daily life. And if that's the case, then shove off, my friend! Away with you!"

Sammy won't admit defeat. "Everybody needs the Lord," he says.

"Maybe so, but you haven't shown me why."

"You're going to die someday, aren't you?"

Simon shrugs. "I don't care."

Sammy turns to the rest of us. "He doesn't care that he's going to die!"

"It's not like it's going to happen this afternoon," Simon says wearily.

"You don't know that."

"Granted, but we can't live as if the Grim Reaper were staring over our shoulders, can we? We'd never get anything done that way. When I say I don't care about dying, I mean it's not high on my list of priorities right now."

A chuckle ripples throughout the bus.

Simon continues. "Now if there's someone on board who's dying of something, they might care about the product you're peddling. But I'm not, so I don't. And I really don't think I'm unique in that respect. Heaven and hell just aren't the urgent topics they used to be in this society. Therefore, you Christians have to change the subject just to get a conversation started about your religion."

Sammy stares off into space, unsure how to regain control of the discussion.

Someone else tries to help. "Are you saying you don't see the relevance of Christianity today?"

Simon points at Sammy. "I'm saying *he* doesn't see

it. And neither do any of the other Christians I've ever talked to. And because *they* don't see it, they can't get *me* to see it. Let me show you what I'm talking about."

He turns to all of us and raises his voice. "How many of you are Christians?"

All around the bus, people hesitate. For one thing, we aren't like Sammy; we don't wear our religion on our sleeves. We're also reluctant to argue with Simon about our faith. Still, quite a number of us raise our hands.

I turn to Savannah and whisper, "More than I would've guessed."

"Good," Simon says. "We might get somewhere. How many of you Christians are going downtown to work this morning?"

Most of us nod or grunt.

"Will Jesus help you?"

We don't know what he means.

"I'll rephrase the question. How many of you can honestly say that God directs your words and actions on the job?"

A few people look like they might be about to make that claim.

"If you answer Yes to that," he adds, "be prepared to give details. Tell us what you have said and done on the job recently that was clearly in response to a divine directive."

Nobody takes him up on it.

"This is precisely my point," Simon concludes. "This bus is full of Christians, yet none of you can claim that your relationship with God has any direct bearing on the work that you're going to do today. Your religion isn't about real life. If there's some connection between your faith and the activities you're about to engage in this morning, you haven't found it."

A white-haired gentleman near the front speaks up. It's our friend Nate. He's the Chief Financial Officer of his company and a very friendly guy. "Everything you say makes perfect sense when applied to fundamentalism," he says. "But there's a lot more to our religion than right-wingers realize. I don't think very much about heaven, either, but I don't need to. My faith in Christ offers me plenty right here and now."

"Like what?" someone asks.

Nate ponders his answer. "Well, I guess I'd have to say 'fellowship.' You can't follow Jesus all by yourself. When you give your life to Him, you become part of His community. I thank God for the people I've had the privilege of worshiping and working with over the years. They've enriched my life in so many ways, I can't count them all."

Simon grimaces. "I just asked all of you whether Christ guides you in the things you do all day, and the answer I got was not encouraging. And now you're saying that the solution to this problem is…?"

Nate smiles. "The church. God's work is done through the church, not through individuals. I give my time and talents to the church, and the church does God's work in the world."

"Can't you see that you're proving my point all over again?" Simon asks. "You're changing the subject, too."

"In what way?"

Simon stares at him in disbelief. "What do you mean, 'In what way'? Apparently none of the Christians on this bus have any idea how their faith applies to their work. I'm asking you what Jesus offers as a solution to this problem, and you tell me it's the pleasure of going to church. I'm asking about Monday through Friday, and you tell me about Sunday."

Nate chuckles. "Well, *my* religion isn't confined to Sunday. I serve on committees that meet on weeknights, and I help out in a number of ways on Saturday. But most importantly, I carry my brothers and sisters in my heart throughout each day and pray for them often. The church is an ever-present reality to me."

"But does it help you do your work better?"

Nate puckers his lips in thought. "Yes," he says. "I think it does. The thought of my fellow believers keeps me striving to do my best throughout the day. It inspires me to be more patient, more compassionate."

Sammy the Soul-Saver has been quiet too long. "Your church sounds like a country club. You hang around with well-to-do people just like you. You all wear fancy clothes, you drive nice cars, and you feel good about yourselves because once in a while you stop to remember those who are less fortunate. When the pastor reads the lesson, you follow along in the pew Bible, and that's the extent of your scripture study. Then you and all your other well-to-do friends head down to Fellowship Hall for coffee and polite conversation. You're just the country-club crowd masquerading as Christians. Jesus is the answer, not your church!"

"You two can argue about that later," Simon says. "My point is still the same: Christians can bring religion to bear on their daily lives only by changing the subject. In your case, that means you're changing the subject to 'the fellowship of the church.' You don't have anything to offer that will make people's daily lives an adventure during working hours. You can suggest nothing better than an after-hours alternative—at best, something to look forward to or reflect back on during the day. But you're still changing the subject. You're turning your thoughts away from your daily business, in another direction. Just because you do it only periodically throughout the day doesn't alter that fact; you're still turning your thoughts *away*. And that shows that your religion doesn't really speak to your daily needs down here in the business district."

A scraggily-looking man sighs impatiently. "All of you are missing the point. You're slaves, every one of you—slaves to the system and to your social roles. You're all so committed to the present world order, you can't even see what's happening."

Simon is delighted. "I haven't had a good argument with a Marxist here in America since the Berlin Wall came down! Where have you been? You and your friends wrung your hands and took cover, and I haven't

7

heard from you since."

"That's a lie and you know it. You may wish you had heard the last of us, but you haven't."

Some people on the bus seem confused, but their neighbors whisper explanations to them. One man says, a little too loudly, "What—he's a communist?"

"I'm a Christian," the scraggily guy says. "I just take my Christianity more seriously than the rest of you do. You *talk* about Christ and his apostles holding their material goods in common. I'm doing something about it."

"Just exactly what are you doing?" someone asks.

"Hastening the revolution," he says. "Opening people's minds. Getting them to see how self-defeating capitalism is."

"What's that got to do with Christianity?"

The guy smiles condescendingly. "What's *capitalism* got to do with Christianity? NOTHING! If you're a Christian, you ought to see that and work to defeat the system. But until then, we must do all we can to relieve the suffering of the homeless and disenfranchised. Those are the very things Jesus would do if He were here."

"Christian Socialists have been around for over a hundred years," Simon explains to us. "A lot of ministers are sympathetic to their ideas—or liberal ministers are, at least. But it's a tough message to preach, especially to wealthy congregations. They squirm too much."

The scraggily guy interrupts. "God is on the side of the poor. That's the thing. You asked these people whether they felt God's direction in their jobs and their lives, and they couldn't give you a straight answer even though they profess to be Christians. The reason is simple: they're godless."

The bus erupts in protest.

"Say what you like, but it's true! God is on the side of those whom society rejects: the poor and the powerless. He has no interest in what you do all day unless you're helping the poor. Sharpen your pencils and balance your ledgers, but don't expect God to care. You're all living lives that are opposed to the work of God. God's only concern is to liberate us all—poor, middle class, and wealthy—from bondage. He's a God of liberation, not of the status quo. As long as you're working for The Powers That Be, you can't expect God's blessing."

A moment of confusion follows as several people try to yell over each other, but Simon restores order. "Once again," he says, "we hear testimony from someone who wants to interest us in the Christian message. And what does he do? He changes the subject."

Turning to the Marxist, Simon continues: "I'm asking how Christ relates to the workplace, and you tell me that the answer is to *eliminate* the workplace as we know it. You don't have a solution to the problem as it stands; you want to avoid the problem altogether and start fresh. That's changing the subject. I concede that Karl Marx recognized what's problematic about the daily lives of working people, but his solution was to change the subject, or rather, to change the structure of society. That kind of answer has always been a tough sell among Americans. Americans want to know what to do here and now to solve their problems. And you have no answer to that question."

Nothing else can be heard after that. Everybody's talking at once. Sammy tries to show the Marxist a Bible passage, but the Marxist shakes his head. Simon gets off the bus, ignoring several people who are fighting for his attention.

Savannah and I look at each other and exhale loudly.

Nate approaches us on his way out. "I've been a Christian all my life," he says, "but I don't know how to respond to something like that." He ponders the matter a moment and finally just shakes his head. "Food for thought," he says, then gets off the bus.

"Maybe so," I tell Savannah. "But right now, I'm choking on it."

2 THE BOTTOM LINE

Savannah and I are not only soul mates; we also work for the same corporation, and we meet for lunch later that day. At the cafeteria, we see D sitting by herself. She invites us to join her.

When Savannah and I started working for the company, D referred to herself as Darla D to distinguish herself from Darla M. Eventually she found this tedious and said, "Just call me DD." But she soon realized that that was redundant, and now she wants us to call her "D." At this rate, pretty soon we won't be calling her anything at all.

Everybody in the building reveres D. She's the director of our department, but we've never met anyone quite so down to earth. She's been with the company for longer than anybody else and knows it inside and out. She's survived major systems changes. She's seen upper level managers come and go. She has implemented sweeping new departmental policies, then she has had to be just as enthusiastic about scrapping them and implementing new ones. She's a strong leader, but she's also a bit of a cynic. Although she welcomes new ideas, she'll make you argue hard for them first.

But what Savannah and I like best about her is her absolute insistence on finding "the bottom line." No matter how confusing an issue may seem to be, she probes and prods until she finds the point of it all. Once she identifies it, she stays with it and will not let the conversation wander from it. Savannah and I have often laughed at Savannah's imitation of D when we've been perplexed about something. "Yes," Savannah says, adopting D's tone of voice, "but let's not lose sight of the bottom line!"

D clears a place for us at the table and asks us how we're doing today. We give the expected answer at first, but then the real story comes out. We tell her what happened on the bus, not omitting a single detail. D listens attentively and does not interrupt. When we're finished, she leans forward slightly. "Let's clarify something," she says.

"It's obvious that this incident has upset both of you. You're reacting to it emotionally. Stop that! You might benefit from the experience if you're willing to do so, but you won't get far by emoting about it. You heard a number of remarks this morning that you didn't like hearing. That doesn't mean they were false. By the same token, it doesn't mean they were true. Your best bet is to get your emotions out of the way and think carefully.

"Now… as I listen to you talk, I don't think you understand why you're so upset. It was an unusual experience, but it shouldn't have rattled you so much. You can't seem to shake it off. Do you know why?"

We shrug, and she continues, "You're troubled by your inability to answer Simon's question. You couldn't accept the answers that other people gave, but you're unable to provide a suitable one of your own."

We think about it a moment, and then we nod.

She smiles reminiscently. "I've been reading a lot to my three-year-old granddaughter," she says. "I've had more than my fill of Clifford the Big Red Dog."

We smile.

"But I've noticed something about Clifford that relates to your problem. In the book, *Clifford's Best Friend*, there's a drawing of Emily Elizabeth in her classroom at school, and another of her doing her homework in her bedroom. Now, Emily Elizabeth has important work to do. She's a student, and it's her job to learn about the world so she can make a contribution to it in some way. There's no getting around it: she has to spend time at school and doing her homework. But both of those pictures are pitiful because, in each one, we see Clifford's eye peering in through the window, waiting. Emily Elizabeth has a job to do, but as long as she's doing it, there's nothing Clifford can do but wait for her to finish. When she's participating in daily life, *Clifford plays no role.* The author, Norman Bridwell, can't think of anything constructive for Clifford to do while Emily Elizabeth is doing her school work. All he can do is wait.

"That's the question you've been asked about today. That's the bottom line."

I glance at Savannah and we try not to laugh.

"Just like Norman Bridwell with Clifford, you can't think of anything constructive God could be doing while you're here in the office. So far as you can see, *God plays no role.* When you're working, all He can do is wait. And that troubles you, because you believe in a God who is actively involved in your lives all the time, no matter what you're doing."

We nod. She's hit the nail on the head, as always.

She continues. "Some folks on the bus offered you alternative solutions, but none of them satisfied you. You weren't impressed by Sammy's assertion that Christ's kingdom is not of this world. Evidently you think God takes an interest in the human race and its secular business: you just don't know what sort of interest. Nor did you find it helpful to say that God works through the institutionalized church rather than through individuals, because you believe that God also works through you as you perform your secular roles. The socialist tried to convince you that you can't be right with God as long as you're grubbing for money. But since you *are* a couple of money-grubbers—and you can't help it any more than Emily Elizabeth can help being a student—then that's no answer at all. Three strikes; you're out. Everybody gets off the bus, and you're left with a big question and no answers."

We nod. "That's pretty much it."

The three of us clean our trays and head down the hall together.

"Personally," she says, "I can't identify with your problem. I don't think of God like you do. You talk like God is an actual Person—a Big Guy in the Sky."

Our faces redden a little. "Well, I wouldn't call God a guy," Savannah says.

"But you do view God as a Person: a Living Being to whom you can talk. You might talk to your bedroom ceiling, but you don't expect it to listen and care about what you're saying. When you talk to God, on the other hand, you do. You believe that He knows you individually and has plans for you. Sort of a CEO of the whole planet."

I consider how to answer this. "I don't know if God is a Person in the same way that a CEO is a person, but I do think He's personal."

She laughs. "You're being evasive. If God isn't a Person, He can't be personal any more than your bedroom ceiling is personal."

We shrug. "Okay. But it sounds like you don't think God is a Person."

"Definitely not," she says. "Too many things just don't add up. There's far too much pain and suffering on this planet to allow me to believe such a thing. If God is in charge of all this, then He's the biggest flop imaginable. I have no respect for anyone who would run the world the way He does. No, I prefer to think that there's a principle of goodness in this world; not a Person, but an active principle working within all living things. Or trying to, anyway. When we heed it, we find some measure of satisfaction and we make the world a better place. When we don't, we make ourselves miserable and ruin the game for everybody else. That's all there is to it, I think. I don't see any reason to make it more complicated than that."

Good ol' D. Always trying to simplify problems—even theological ones.

We reach the door of her office and she pauses. "That's what it comes down to, you know. If you insist on believing that God is a Person and you feel you must stay in close contact with this Person all day and all night, then you've got to figure out what role He's playing even when you're busy doing other things."

She shakes her head and walks away humming "The Impossible Dream."

3 A.P.B.

That night, we decide to ask for help online. We post a note to all our friends, telling them what we're trying to do. We describe our experience on the bus and we mention our conversation with D.

"In a nutshell," we write, "we're trying to answer the question, 'What does God do from 9 to 5?' If you have any ideas or you know someone who does, we'd appreciate your input."

We get a flood of responses. Some are brief and silly.

"He watches daytime television."

"He runs the carpenters' union."

Others are pious but unhelpful.

"God holds the planets in their courses and keeps everything working the way it's supposed to. Imagine what chaos there would be if God wasn't sustaining the universe! The air we breathe, gravity—everything is a gift from God to us, renewed each day."

Several people email us the "Footprints in the Sand"

poem. Nobody gives a detailed, substantive answer to the question.

Savannah and I shake our heads. "Maybe nobody knows."

Our friend Harley writes that God is in the business of saving souls. "Our jobs offer opportunities for us to share our testimony of Christ with coworkers or clients. That's all that really matters from God's perspective. Don't make the mistake of turning work into a religion!"

We reply, "Don't worry, Harley, that's not our intention. But on your view, most of the things we do all day are of no spiritual concern. We have to work for a living, but the things we do to earn our living are themselves of little value. We must be content knowing that our work provides us with opportunities for sharing our testimony with others—nothing more. Never mind that the largest share of our time therefore goes toward meaningless tasks. We must perform those tasks patiently, always looking for opportunities to do what's really important: to talk about the Lord.

"Sorry, but that just sounds like a restatement of the problem, not a solution to it. According to your view, there's no help for anyone who makes productive contributions to this world and longs to share the experience with God."

His reply is short and to the point: "What could be more productive than to spread the gospel?"

"We're surprised we have to spell this out," we reply. "Just to survive in this world, we're forced every day to rely on the competence and vigilance of large numbers of people we've never met. We expect the engineers to pay attention when they install our elevators. We expect the folks at the telephone company to route our calls properly. We expect the people at the water purification plant to give us clean water. And so on. If any of these people don't do their jobs, we're all going to suffer.

"It's not a question of whether the secular roles we play are important. The question is whether they are important *to God*. We find it necessary, for everyone's sake, to engage in such employments today. But is it possible for us to discover spiritual meaning in these activities? Or must we be content to live a divided life, spending only some of our time in religious pursuits and spending much more of it performing the productive work that our society requires of us?"

Harley says he understands what we're saying. "But the hard truth is, God doesn't care about the work we do all day. Work, after all, is a product of our fall from the Garden of Eden. You want something you can't have. God does call us to an adventure in the workplace, but the adventure isn't the work itself. We're called to the adventure of saving souls. Remember what Christ Himself did when He found people working: He called them to leave their fishing nets and their accounting tables and follow Him. We can't improve on His message."

We thank Harley for his input. We agree that saving souls is part of what God does all day. "But we think there's more to it than that. We believe in a God who is very involved in the details of our daily lives. We just can't quite put our fingers on what it is God is doing about those details."

Among the other responses we've received, Paula's is especially interesting. She suggests that God's influence is most obvious in a well-developed conscience. "The secular details of our daily lives are important to God because they have ethical implications," she writes. "Just when we think we're doing something utterly private, it often has consequences for our coworkers, our clients, our loved ones, or society at large."

We tell Paula that we've been thinking the same thing, but we aren't entirely satisfied with that answer. The problem is, ethics doesn't cover everything we do on the job. In fact, it doesn't even cover the most important things.

"Take engineering, for example. Yes, engineers have immense moral obligations. They're accountable for public safety as well as for maintaining the well-being of our environment. But the substance of what they do all day is mathematical. They solve problems involving abstract concepts like acceleration, absolute zero temperature, and magnetic flux. Is God interested in such problems? If we say No, then that would mean that God overlooks the most important aspects of an engineer's daily life. And it's difficult to see how God could pass judgment on an engineer's ethics without taking these abstract problems into consideration. But if

can't agree that it's a full integration. Brother Lawrence doesn't seem to have discussed recipes with God, for example! He just kept his mind on God while he was cooking. Yes, this helped him maintain his composure, which in turn aided him in order-taking. But we're striving for something more substantial than this."

We tell him about D's example of Clifford the Big Red Dog peering in at Emily Elizabeth while she's in school. "In our experience, practicing the presence amounts to looking up at the window constantly throughout the day and seeing God smiling upon us. We derive a certain amount of inner peace from this exercise, but we sense that we could be getting so much more from the interaction than this. It all comes down to the question D posed: Does God play any role when we're in the office, or is He just observing? What, in other words, does God *do* from 9 to 5?"

"Hm," Phil says. "Don't know. But I'll ask Him for you."

"Let us know what He says," we reply.

Not everyone is as good-natured as Phil. Joan writes that she didn't appreciate getting our email. "What in the world are you talking about?" she asks. She says our question is deeply offensive.

"I work hard and I earn a decent wage. I live a good Christian life. I'm an ethical person. With the money I earn, I give a lot to the church and to charitable organizations. What more do you want from me? I resent your implication that I'm not a good Christian just because I don't turn it all over to God."

"I guess we'll have to talk to her in person," Savannah says.

Carl isn't insulted, but he, too, considers the question ridiculous. "You seem to think that God micromanages," he writes. "Like He wants us to consult Him before we do anything, all day long. I could never accept a religion like that. God put a good head on my shoulders and He trusts me to make my own decisions."

I turn to Savannah and sigh. "I'm starting to regret that we sent out this message. Nobody seems to understand what we're trying to do."

Then Cameron, one of our coworkers, texts us. "Have you ever heard of Grizzled Mane?"

We think a minute. "Is it a hair salon?"

She sends us a laughing emoticon. "Dr. Grizzled Mane is Philosopher-in-Residence at the Cathedral of Our Lord, downtown."

"C.O.O.L.," we reply.

"Exactly! What you two are talking about is the very thing he specializes in. I visit the Cathedral every now and then when I need a fresh perspective. I'm never disappointed."

We ask her several questions at once. Who is he? What's his approach?

"Well, he's an ordained minister, although he's not one of the pastors. He's got a doctorate in philosophy. He's funny and entertaining, but he also makes you think."

"About what?" we ask. "What kinds of things does he say?"

"Well, for example, he says that anybody who believes in the Argument from Design must believe that God is interested in secular subjects."

I answer her. "The Argument from Design says that the universe is too well-ordered not to have been created by an Intelligent Designer. So he's saying...?"

"That if you accept that argument then it's inconsistent to treat God as if He were only interested in religion. If God is a Grand Designer, then He must care an awful lot about chemistry, physics, biology, geoscience, and lots of other subjects."

"Does Dr. Mane only talk about science?" Savannah asks.

"No. He says the main spiritual problem these days is the fact that we have trouble finding God in the things we do all day. That's his favorite subject."

I'm excited. "We'd like to talk to him."

"No problem. He leads an informal discussion in the cathedral parlor on Wednesday evenings. Everybody's welcome. He doesn't come with a script. He asks you what's on your mind and he discusses it with you."

"Perfect!" I say. "Can't wait."

"I wish I could go," Cameron says, "but I'll be busy tomorrow night. One word of advice: don't be shocked. He may have a PhD, but that parlor group is a tough crowd. They often disagree with him, and they can be pretty vocal about it sometimes. I call him the Rodney

Dangerfield of religious philosophers."

I look at Savannah and smirk. "Sounds like every church I've ever been in. It's always open season when it comes to criticizing the minister!"

"Hm," says Savannah. "But to his face? Sounds scary. Still… I really want to hear what he's got to say."

4 'GRIZZLED' IS AN UNDERSTATEMENT

There are no gargoyles on the roof of the Cathedral of Our Lord. It's such a huge, forbidding structure, I always assumed the little monsters were there. I distinctly remember making jokes about them with my friends, asking why anybody would put such fiends on the roof of a church. We all laughed. Now it turns out there aren't any. Oops.

As Savannah and I enter the huge lobby doors, I wonder if we really will be welcome like Cameron says. We're not rich or famous, and lots of rich and famous people go to this church. Joe Fiske, owner of the Fiske supermarket chain, is a member here. So is Katie Carruthers of Channel 7 news. I could go on, but Savannah's already rolling her eyes, so I decide to shut up.

Crossing the spacious lobby, we catch a glimpse of

the softly-lit sanctuary, so we step in to take a better look. Our mouths drop open. It's more than just huge and beautiful. There's a feeling here that we can't quite describe. It's like we've stepped into a larger world.

"Wow!" Savannah whispers.

"Yeah..."

A young lady greets us companionably. We tell her why we've come, and she escorts us down the hall to The Parlor: a room full of comfortable furniture and a large fireplace. A varied assortment of people are already gathered and busily chatting. Some look like they have a lot of money, but most of them are young and unassuming like us. They welcome us and show us where the coffee and tea are, but nobody asks us if we're members or if we're interested in becoming members. Apparently many of them are newcomers, too. We meet an aerospace engineer and a marketing analyst.

"Be sure to log onto the Water Cooler Club tomorrow," somebody tells us. "It's a chat room. It gives us all a chance to continue the discussion we started tonight."

A friendly lady with a shock of silver hair shakes our hands. "I'm Noreen Butler, but people around here call me NB."

"She's our in-house reference librarian," a man tells us. "A walking bibliographical miracle. Just wait— you'll see!"

In all our conversations, people keep mentioning GM and I can't figure out why. Finally I whisper to

Savannah, "Why is everybody talking about General Motors?"

"Are they?"

"Yes. They keep saying GM this, GM that."

She looks at me and pauses a moment for effect, then says, very slowly, "Dr. *Grrr*izzled *Mmmm*ane."

"Ohhhhh."

As if on cue, GM enters the room. He's slightly overweight with wire rim glasses, white hair, and a beard. He's squeezing shoulders and shaking hands.

"He reminds me of somebody," I tell Savannah.

She grins. "Someone rich and famous?"

"That depends. Do you consider Santa Claus rich or just famous?"

She looks horrified. "Please don't embarrass me."

But it's true. And her suppressed laugh proves it.

Everybody finds a seat. After briefly seeking a divine blessing upon our conversation, Santa—GM, that is— asks us what we want to talk about tonight. There's a moment's hesitation, so I raise my hand. Savannah looks like she doesn't quite trust me, but it's too late. GM invites me to speak.

"A friend of ours recently posed a problem to us in the form of a homey analogy. She's been reading a lot of Clifford books to her grandchild and she's noticed that Clifford has nothing to do while Emily Elizabeth is in school." I pause a moment and turn to the rest of the group. "Sorry… is everyone familiar with Clifford?"

Apparently they are. So is Santa.

31

I continue. "Our friend compared Clifford to God, because there are often times in which Clifford's giant eye stares in at Emily Elizabeth while she's studying. This seemed to our friend to be analogous to the idea of an omniscient God watching us all as we do our daily work. Our friend pointed out that, in both cases, there doesn't seem to be anything left for the observing party to do except to observe." I turn back to GM. "We'd like to hear what you think."

Heads nod in interest, and people whisper to each other all around the room.

GM is delighted. "Wonderful!" he says. "Fascinating analogy! And what a challenge!"

Savannah adds, "We were thinking of phrasing the question this way: What does God do from 9 to 5?"

"9 to 5!" someone protests. "What if you work the night shift?"

"Or weekends?" says another.

"Or part-time?"

"Or around the clock?"

But GM laughs. "Now, now! We all know what '9 to 5' means. Of course, nobody has ever actually worked an 8-hour day from 9 to 5, unless they skipped lunch."

Savannah turns to me and raises an eyebrow warily.

"Tough crowd," I remind her. "But I like it."

GM's wheels are turning. "Our challenge is to express in words what it is that God does while we're busily engaged in secular pursuits. But let's not be so hasty about dismissing the image of God as an observer.

It would be a marvelous thing to be able to see 'The Big Picture.' I've often wished that I could catch just a glimpse of the activity that takes place in a single day in this city.

"Think of it! What if there were a magical observation booth somewhere in the heart of town where you could see everybody all at once?"

"Like a giant ant farm?" somebody asks.

"Somewhat. Except you don't just see the mass of people—like so many ants—but you can pick out each one individually. You can also tell what they're thinking and feeling. You know what they want and what they fear. You're aware of their stresses and strains."

"Sounds a little like Reality TV," someone says.

"I'm not so sure" he replies. "Reality TV is greatly edited and served up to us in a digestible form. In this magical observation booth, on the other hand, we have intimate, inside knowledge of all that's happening in all its complexity, all at once, and in a single glance. When we step into this observation booth, we can see people everywhere, doing what they do all day. Wouldn't it be an awesome thing to have such depth and scope of vision?"

Nobody says anything. We're all thinking.

"Join me in trying to visualize this for a minute. What kinds of work environments would we be able to see from this magical observation booth?"

The room is quiet a moment, then people speak up.

"Factories."

"High-rise office buildings."

"Department stores."

"Gas stations."

"The halls of justice—and jails and prisons."

"Schools," a teenager adds. "Well, you know. Speaking of prisons."

Everybody laughs.

GM chuckles but is thoughtful. "Any place of employment can become a prison easily enough. But you're right to include schools in this list. You students are working people, too. The school is your workplace."

"Maybe I should ask for a raise," the kid says.

GM turns to the rest of us. "Where else do people work?"

"Outside," someone says. "I'm thinking of highway construction crews."

"Speaking of highways," someone else adds, "there are professional drivers like truckers. Their cabs form their actual work environment."

"Taxi cabs!" says another. "And police cars. And buses, trains, and subways."

The list keeps growing. We mention hospitals, airplanes and airline terminals, fishing boats, barges, ocean liners, mine shafts, barber shops and boutiques, restaurants, theaters, call centers, fitness clubs.

"Fine!" GM says. "Now… we step into our magical observation booth and we watch all this activity going on. What a sight! Imagine perceiving all the connections, all the interrelationships." He points to imaginary spots all around him. "Here are factory workers building parts. Those parts are shipped by *this* trucker over *that* stretch of highway that was just recently repaired by *this* construction crew. The supervisor of the crew has a question, so he's talking on a cell phone to someone in *this* call center over here. The lady he's talking to puts him on hold and calls an engineer at *that* office building.

"Remember, we're not only able to see all this but also to tell what all these people are thinking and feeling. So besides the vast machinery of all these professional relationships, we catch the drama and pathos of the scene in all its complexity. We mortals are not able to view life from such an exalted vantage point, but imagine if we could!"

"That would be interesting to see," someone admits, "but I'm not getting your point."

"Just this," he says, and he gestures to me. "There's a crucial disanalogy between God's observation of us and Clifford's observation of Emily Elizabeth. While she's in school, Clifford can do nothing but sit and wait—and whine. But God's observation of us is active; it's full of understanding. It makes connections, recognizes problems and their causes, sees possibilities. Even if God were doing nothing more than observing us, that would still be a lot more than Clifford is doing. Clifford is just waiting for Emily Elizabeth to get out of school so he can interact with her again. God is *doing* something."

I nod. "I can see that, and I admit that the analogy isn't as close as it seemed to me when our friend presented it to us. But what you describe God as doing still falls short of a lively interaction with us. And the end result is that, while we're at work, God seems to play no role."

"Yes," he agrees, "that *is* how it seems so far. I realize I haven't answered your question yet. And I'm afraid it's going to take me all night to do so!"

Everybody who knows him laughs. "Ain't *that* the truth!"

"But before I get started, I want us to realize that God's observation of us is not as passive as it may seem. And that's an important point—a crucial one, I think. I'll be coming back to it before we're finished."

He turns back to the group. "So… what does God do all day? That's the question we've set out to answer."

"Should we consult the scriptures?" someone suggests.

"Definitely! But first, let's get a better focus on the question. The problem begins on the secular side. We don't have an adequate understanding of what *we* are doing from 9 to 5. We think we do, but we're too close to it and don't often take time to analyze what's happening. I invite you now to look at secular life with new eyes. In doing so, I believe you'll see that there's much more to it than you've ever realized."

wrong and learn from our mistakes."

"Or not," somebody says again.

"Or not," GM agrees. "And then the story continues. But back to my main point: this fundamental competency is a subplot in the overall story of our lives, and this subplot alone is incredibly complicated."

Someone says, "I'm trying to follow the direction of your thought, but I'm a little confused. So far, this sounds like a child development class. Are you saying that who we are now was all decided in the first dozen years of our lives?"

"Not at all. I'm saying that we were being formed and shaped even in those earliest days, but many storylines continue into adulthood and even beyond. Let me give you some other examples that illustrate this."

He thinks a moment. "There's the story of how we learned to converse. It may seem like a simple thing, but this story alone is immense.

"As small children, we lacked the vocabulary to express much of what was on our minds. We liked to keep the conversation focused on ourselves. We had a short attention span, either jumping from one subject to another or dropping out of the discussion altogether if something else caught our interest.

"Over time our vocabulary grew, our attention span increased, and we recognized the value of talking about topics other than ourselves; but we still had many sub-skills to master. It wasn't enough just to listen to the other person; we had to learn not to finish their sentences for them, not to interrupt, and not even to assume that we knew where the conversation was headed. Surprisingly, it was sometimes hard to know exactly what the other person was trying to say. It was also difficult at times to get the other person to understand what *we* were saying, especially when we were joking or when we used what we assumed was a common expression or figure of speech. Sometimes we were embarrassed to learn that we had been using a word or phrase incorrectly. We learned by doing—again and again, day after day after day.

"And then there were points of conversational etiquette. We found ways to suppress a yawn when the other person was speaking. We learned to gauge when we were talking too much, and if so then we stopped and let the other person have their chance. We discovered the correct distance at which to stand when conversing with another person—not too close, not too far. We picked up clues about proper voice tone, volume, speed, pitch. We learned to avoid staring when the other person had food lodged between his teeth. We developed strategies of self-preservation when he had bad breath.

"We also learned that there were many styles of conversation and that we must not confuse them. Topics that were appropriate in the locker room were not welcome at mom's sewing circle. An impersonal demeanor was just right when giving an oral report on the history of the Stamp Act, but it failed to do the job on a first date. We were entitled to speak sharply to the person who plowed into our new car, but we had better not talk that way to our boss.

"All of us reached our current patterns of conversational behavior as a result of an immense and complex story: the story of all the conversations we've ever had. But the ability to converse effectively is just one of many skills that are necessary for living competent and happy lives. We take these skills for granted and don't think of them as important subplots in the story of our lives, but they are. All of these skills are essential, and each took time to develop. Each represents a subplot in the story of how we became who we are right now. In the case of conversational skills, we're all still learning from day to day, even when we're old.

"But you yourselves can probably come up with even more vivid examples of how these storylines continue on even in adulthood. How many of you have gone through significant changes in outlook over the last several years?"

A number of people share their stories. A young woman tells about how she wanted to advance in her company. "It was all about *me* at first," she says. "But before long I became a manager, and then I started caring much more about the people who reported to me. Instead of thinking just about myself and my own advancement, I began to think much more about my department as a whole. Becoming a manager changed me. What I want now is not the same thing I wanted five years ago."

"We had a similar situation in our marriage," a young couple confesses. "We went into our relationship thinking only about each other. We spent long hours listening to each other and understanding each other's needs. Then we had a child, and everything changed. Now the main topic of conversation is our little boy— when we're lucky enough to have a conversation. *His* needs are what really matter to us now."

"I'm single," says a woman in her thirties, "but I recently became a homeowner. It's amazing how a simple thing like that can change you in so many ways! Now I have neighbors to think about, a lawn to mow, leaky faucets to fix, creaky doors to lubricate, and a mortgage to pay off. Sometimes I look back longingly to those carefree days when I lived in an apartment. But I wouldn't give up my home for anything!"

After several more testimonials like these, GM sums up. "We can go on and on. Retirement brings all new problems and opportunities. The emptying of the nest (or our failure to do so) can make profound changes in us. Travel, illness, the adoption of new leisure activities all make their marks on us. We never stop facing new challenges in life, whether we want to or not. The aging process alone brings new experiences. Even the strongest among us must deal eventually with some form of enfeeblement. We discover new concerns, new ways of seeing life, new means, new ends. All of these can be considered subplots in the overall story of our life. And when we put all the subplots together, the story is immense.

"Devotional writers often approach everyday life as if it were actually quite simple. They attract readers with homey titles like *Life's Little Instruction Manual* or *All I Ever Needed to Know about Life I Learned in Kindergarten*.

"I love those books!" somebody says.

"Lots of people do," GM admits. "They contain some good insights, but I disagree with their main thesis. In each case, they offer a few simple, general principles for getting along in the world. They tell us that the key to happiness is to cut through the apparent complexity of modern life by keeping a few simple principles in mind. And that's the point at which I disagree.

"Sometimes we even hear this message from the pulpit. I once read a transcript of a sermon like this. The pastor imagined what would happen if Jesus were to appear at his doorstep one afternoon. The answer: he and the Lord would go out to the lake and skip stones across the water. As the pastor's stone skips the surface three times, Christ turns to him and says, 'Hey, you're good.'"

We laugh.

"The point of the sermon was that the Master wants us to slow down, to enjoy life, to put aside the hustle-bustle and live simply. Furthermore, the sermon implied that it's the simple things of life that really matter to God. If we were to hear what God thinks of our everyday life, we'd discover Him calling us back to basics. Slow down. Relax. Stop fretting about the details.

They don't really matter in the larger scheme of things. It seems to me that this is exactly the wrong approach to finding God in everyday life."

A gray-haired man interrupts with a wry smile. "You don't believe in KISS?"

GM looks at him uncomprehendingly.

"KISS. You know: 'Keep It Simple, Stupid.'"

"Actually," GM says, "that's a good rule of thumb in most cases. We often make things harder than they need to be. Since we're creatures of limited intelligence, it's usually best for us to simplify situations as much as possible in order to understand them. But in this case— when we're trying to understand what the Divine Mind is doing in our lives every day—it is of utmost importance that we recognize the complexity of the situation. The Divine Mind does not have the limitations that our minds have. It's precisely by trying to 'Keep It Simple' that we've failed to see God's activity in our lives.

"At any rate, do you see now why I said that we don't really know much about ourselves?"

I nod. "Yes, because most of what has happened to us has passed us by without our even noticing it. Some of it we did notice at the time but have since forgotten. Compared to the entire scope of our experience, what we are now able to remember about our lives is extremely sketchy. However, who we are now is the result of the whole story and not just the fragments that we remember of it."

"Perfect!" he replies. "Perhaps in the future I should tell my answers to you and you can summarize them for the group. We'll get out of here hours earlier that way."

Someone interrupts. "GM, it seems to me that you've been side-stepping the nature/nurture issue. It sounds like you're assuming that we're shaped by our experience and that our genetic makeup doesn't come into play at all. But that point is much too controversial for you to assume without supporting your position."

GM's eyes light up. "Thanks for that feedback. That shows me I'm not getting my point across."

He turns to the rest of us. "Is everyone familiar with the nature/nurture problem?"

Most of us seem to be, but a few are non-committal, so he explains briefly. "This is a debate that's been going on at least since the early 1600s. Shakespeare mentions it in *The Tempest*."

NB adds immediately: "Act 4, Scene 1, lines 188 to 190."

Savannah and I smile at each other.

GM continues. "Some people think that we were born the way we are: stubborn or accommodating, malicious or kind, flighty or serene. According to this view, we are who we are by *nature*. Others say we're the product of our environment. The way we're raised and the experiences we undergo determine how we'll turn out. According to this view, we are who we are because of the way we were *nurtured*. I've just been informed that I've been speaking as if I believed in nurture over nature."

The person who asked the question explains. "You keep saying that we are who we are as a result of all that we've experienced. In other words, you sound like you're coming down on the side of nurture."

"I see," says GM. "Apparently I haven't given adequate emphasis to the fact that we're all actively engaged in this process. The problem with each of these options—either nature or nurture—is that they're both essentially passive. On the former view, we're made who we are by our genetic inheritance; on the latter view, by the things that happen to us. Either way, we can't help ourselves. We are who we are because of what's been done to us by forces beyond our control.

"I've always felt that the question itself is much too simplistic—and yes, once again I think we would do better *not* to 'Keep It Simple' in this case. Forgive the digression, but I think I should spend a few minutes clarifying what I've said so far, relative to this nature/nurture problem. Then we'll be closer to answering the main question of the night: what God does from 9 to 5."

6 NATURE? NURTURE? NEITHER?

"Let me rephrase what I've been saying so that I emphasize the active rather than the passive," GM suggests. "Who we are at this moment in our lives is the result of everything we've said, done, and thought so far. From the moment we were born, we've been on the move, wanting lots of different kinds of things and taking many different courses of action to achieve our wants. Notice what I'm emphasizing this time: that we're active human beings, not sitting ducks.

"Now, at every phase of our lives from birth 'til death, there are innumerable things we *could* want; but in fact, there is a limited range of things we actually *do* want. I myself have no interest in wearing a chinchilla coat, driving a Harley Davidson, or running a triathlon, but there are lots of people who do want such things. Although we each may have many desires, our range of desires is really quite limited compared to the innumerable possibilities life presents.

"What limits us? There may be other factors, but the two we were just discussing are the most obvious: our genetic predispositions and our experience so far. Let's start with genetics. We may have a built-in tendency to favor bright colors over pastels. Or we may prefer quiet, reflective activities over loud, boisterous ones. Or we may naturally lean in the direction of shooting first and asking questions later. I'm not saying that we're programmed to act in these ways all the time, under every circumstance; if that were true, then we'd be nothing more than creatures of instinct—which apparently we're not. We're born with propensities, but we do deviate from them sometimes, too.

"But it's not just our desires that are influenced by genetics. Obviously, we're born with certain abilities and disabilities. I, for example, could never have become an opera singer or a trapeze artist. My talents are such that these would never have been real possibilities for me even if I had gotten it into my head to try them. So the innumerable possibilities that life presents to us are narrowed down considerably by our genetic endowments... or the lack thereof.

"The other important limiting factor is our environment. In some cases our environment acts in concert with our natural dispositions and in other cases it acts in opposition to them. For example, we may be born with a natural desire to observe group activities rather than to participate. But if our parents, siblings, friends, and teachers all exert strong pressure on us to participate, then we will probably overcome our natural tendency to hang back. On the other hand, if the people in our environment are tolerant of our desire to withdraw—or especially if they encourage that kind of behavior by being overly critical of our mistakes—then our built-in desire will be reinforced by our experience, and we will very likely grow up standoffish.

"I think it's best to view nature and nurture as factors which, together, define the options available to us. They don't make us who we are; they do, however, limit the range of our potential projects. Instead of wanting everything imaginable, we have a limited range of wants in life, based on both our inborn tendencies and the opportunities offered by our environment. And out of the range of things we want, only some things are really possible, either because of our genetic endowments or because of our environmental limitations. In some cases our environment influences us more heavily than our genetic instructions; in other cases the reverse is true; in still other cases the two work together. Nevertheless, we're not mere putty in the hands of these two factors. Our active engagement with our environment, again and again throughout all the events of our lives so far, has brought us to this moment."

A woman interrupts. "When you speak in the singular like this—'*the* environment'—it sounds as if we live our entire lives within one single set of circumstances. But the fact is, we move in and out of many environments: home, neighborhood, school, church, workplace. And, in each of these, the dynamics change over time. The family changes as new members are added or as each child matures. Neighborhoods change as families come and go. A school can seem friendly to a child one year and become a House of Horrors the next, depending on who the teacher is and who the child's classmates are."

GM nods. "That's an excellent point. We speak of 'the environment' for simplicity's sake. Once again, life turns out to be much more complex than we usually acknowledge. This is precisely why some of you mentioned having new experience lately as managers, newlyweds, parents, or homeowners. A change in any of these environments offers new possibilities for us. Suddenly we're able—or perhaps even required—to do things that were not serious possibilities for us before."

The new homeowner speaks up. "I've got a great example of that. I've never had any interest in insects, but my home changed me."

"In what way?" he asks her.

"Not long after I moved in, I started noticing perfectly round holes drilled into the bottom of my deck. I was very upset at first, and I couldn't figure out where they were coming from. Then a friend of mine pointed out that I had bees in my deck. I'd never heard of such a thing. Bees that drill into the wood and live in your deck! Can you imagine! They're called carpenter bees!"

"Were they union or non-union?" somebody quips.

"The thing is, I was surprised by my reaction. Instead of just wanting them dead and out of my wood, I began learning about them. Then I started noticing the other insects that passed through my yard. For the first time in my life, I wondered about fireflies and butterflies. I checked out books about the various kinds of insects and learned about their habits. Now insect-watching is my newest hobby. I never would've guessed that I'd care about such a thing."

GM nods. "We can never predict how a shift in one of our environments will change our interests. And this drives home the point once again that we don't know ourselves as thoroughly as we think we do.

"At any rate, this is the best answer I can give to the nature/nurture question. When I say that we are who we are because of the entire story of everything we've experienced so far, I don't mean to say that we've been passively shaped by our experience. Rather, I mean that we've been molded by our active engagement with our environments—plural, not singular. Who we are at this moment is the outcome of all the stories of all of our hopes and dreams, all the things we've tried to do, all the things we've said, as well as all the things we've seen and heard others do—and the reactions we've had to all these experiences. It's much too simplistic to say that the determining factor is either our natural propensities or our environment. Ultimately, we are who we are because of all the choices we've made within the limited range of possibilities that nature and nurture have allowed us to consider, as well as the outcomes of those choices and how we chose to react to those outcomes.

"The thing I want to emphasize most of all is the immensity of it. We're all so caught up in this patchwork quilt of stories that we can't possibly see it all and analyze it in its entirety. It's too big, too complex. And yet our development proceeds, even though we aren't capable of comprehending it all. We don't have to understand it or even be aware of it in order for it to move ahead. We're constantly evolving whether we know it or not."

7 HOW WE GO WRONG

"Now…" he continues, "when we reflect on the complexity of our development as individuals, we can see that there is ample room for each of us to chart out our own unique paths in life. In every episode of each of these subplots, we make choices that define us. There is also plenty of opportunity to go wrong, or at least to fall short of all that we could be.

"For example, as children, perhaps we spoke too frankly on occasion, but our remarks drew such negative reactions from adults that we eventually learned to keep at least some of our opinions to ourselves. But imagine a little boy who never learns this lesson. His parents think he's a prodigy and they encourage him to speak his mind, even though he's mean-spirited. Often his remarks hurt his playmates' feelings. He even speaks offensively to adults. But his parents laugh and applaud him. As he grows to manhood, he prides himself on his stark honesty. 'I tell it like it is,' he says.

"Unfortunately, people often treat him coolly and he can't understand why. He consoles himself with the thought that people don't like him because he tells it like it is."

"Why would anybody want to be around him?" someone asks. "He probably comes across as superior."

GM nods. "This is a hypothetical case, of course, but in the scenario I'm describing, he does act superior. And most people are either turned off or intimidated. Once in a while he meets people who are kindly disposed toward him and aren't afraid to talk back to him. They try to give him constructive criticism, but he won't listen. Although he's always been brutally honest with others, he can't accept criticism himself."

"He can dish it out but he can't take it," somebody comments.

"Of course he can't," says someone else. "He's never learned how."

GM nods again. "Right. That's one storyline he managed to skip. He's had a lot of practice telling other people how things look to him, but he's had almost no experience hearing how things look to others. He doesn't know how to process that kind of information, especially if it conflicts with his own self-perception. So he brushes off the criticism and goes on 'telling it like it is' to everybody else.

"You can well imagine the ramifications this will have in his personal and professional life."

People jump in. "No friends, probably."

"Or at least not many."

"Unlucky in love."

"Oh, he'll find love. Some poor girl will believe his song and dance. She'll treat him like a god and he'll treat her like dirt. Next thing you know, she'll be trapped. And she won't have the brains or the guts to get out of the relationship. Happens all the time."

"He'll probably get passed up for promotions. Even if he's good at what he does, he's liable to ruffle too many feathers. Nobody will put in a good word for him."

"Or even if they do, he'll be difficult to work with."

"And he's probably not any good at networking."

GM tries not to laugh. "Remember, though, that life is much more complex than this. I've described only one of his character traits. He's gone through many other storylines and has developed an entire ensemble of traits besides this one. Don't make him out to be *all* bad!"

"Well," somebody says, "it's hard to get around arrogance. If he insults people, there's little else you can tell us about him that'll make him seem likeable."

"All right," GM replies, accepting the challenge. "Let's say he's extremely kind to those who are less fortunate. He's the rare soul who stops on the street corner and converses with the homeless. When he's introduced to children, he kneels down to talk to them. When he's at a family gathering and great-great-grandma is sitting in the corner by herself, he goes and sits with her. And he's extremely respectful towards women and fights for their rights every chance he gets."

Half the people in the room change their attitude. "Doesn't sound so bad after all."

"Exactly," GM replies. "That's the trouble. He knows he's a good person. And he's got plenty of evidence to back up his conviction. Unfortunately he has this one glaring personality flaw that shuts him off from others, and he can't see it."

The new homeowner thinks out loud, "I'll bet the same thing could be said about any one of us! We have our own perceptions of ourselves, and maybe they're fairly accurate overall, but we might have some glaring fault that we've blinded ourselves to. And if our friends and family don't tell us, we might never find out!"

GM is delighted at this confession. "At the very least, all of us have room to grow in a variety of ways that we may not recognize. Even if we don't have glaring faults, all of us have room for improvement. Despite all the worthwhile traits we've acquired, there are always going to be some others we could've acquired but didn't. And we all arrived at these shortcomings in the same way: by failing to learn some of the lessons that we could've potentially learned along the way. It may be that our experience has been limited in certain respects, preventing us from going through episodes that would've made it possible for us to learn those lessons. Or maybe we did go through those episodes but we didn't learn all that we could've learned from them."

Someone protests. "But our life experience doesn't

come labeled. We have to draw our own conclusions as we go along. How can we know what we're supposed to learn from a given episode?"

"That's just it," GM says. "Each episode contains so many possible lessons, we may not learn them all. Maybe we learned some things and skimmed over others. Precisely because the lessons *aren't* spelled out for us, it's highly unlikely that we *will* learn all we can possibly learn from a given experience. The result? You and I each have many opportunities for growth, even though we can also point to many victories. We humans are so incredibly rich in potential that it's possible for us to have many strengths and yet have many weaknesses, too."

"Who cares?" someone asks. "Nobody's perfect."

"Again, that's the problem. We do have to draw the line somewhere. Out of an indefinite number of possibilities for growth, we learn what we can and we hope for the best. And we might be successful at living a happy and productive life, even though we don't become all that we possibly could've become. Sadly, however, many of us succeed at living only *somewhat* happily or only *partially* productively—and we don't know why. As humans, we lack the mental equipment to scan our massive life histories and recall the lessons we failed to learn.

"This is another case in which devotional writers paint an overly simplistic picture. They often talk as if we can point to a single fork in the road—a decisive moment in which we chose evil rather than good. It's not that simple. We've arrived where we are today by means of all of our actions and reactions in all the episodes of our vast life history. We came through some of these episodes heroically, others not so well. But most of what happened is forgotten.

"Now let's return to the young man who 'tells it like it is.' The first point I want to make is this: that he wasn't born this way, even though his arrogance is deeply-ingrained. He's the way he is because of—"

"—all the stories of all the things he's experienced so far," we chime in.

"I guess I've made my point," he mutters.

"And then some," we reply.

He clears his throat. "Let's move on to the next point, then. *If this young man is ever going to change, it will be as a result of new storylines—new experiences that will reach him in a way that his previous storylines have not.*

"People have tried to get him to listen before and have been unsuccessful. He wasn't ready to hear what they had to say. The criticism came at a time in his overall life story when the situation didn't reinforce it, didn't drive it home. But as trite as this may sound, there's always hope—always a chance that new experience will make him aware of his shortcomings. It's highly unlikely, of course, but it's at least possible."

Savannah interjects. "Can you give an example?"

He hands the question back to the group. "Here's a young man who is often rude to others and does it in the name of honesty—of 'telling it like it is.' Can anyone think of storylines that could make this young man stop acting like this?"

People throw out suggestions.

"Maybe if he really wants to be friends with somebody and is refused. I know it's happened already and he didn't take the hint, but maybe if he meets someone he really wants to be friends with and they're turned off by him and tell him so, maybe that'll make him stop and think."

"Or let's say he's the obvious candidate for a promotion and he's counting on it. Then they pass over him and tell him why. Maybe that'll sink in."

"Or he falls in love. He totally loses his heart to a woman, and she turns him down."

Someone interjects. "You're all taking a negative approach. I like this guy. Sure, he's got a major flaw in his character, but I want to see him succeed. Isn't there something good that could happen to him, that would make him stop and think?"

"That's just what I was wondering," someone else says. "Let's have him meet the love of his life, and she loves him in return. He worships the ground she walks on. And she tells him, 'Look, I love ya, but you better straighten up or this'll never work out.' And he says, 'What are you talking about?' And she tells him. At first, he thinks she's wrong, but he loves her so much, he listens. And before long, he begins to realize that she's right."

Someone gags. "That's too mushy for me. Even a guy like this must have somebody he looks up to. Let's say he idolizes the VP of his company. One day the VP calls him in and says, 'Look, you gotta stop insulting your associates.' And he says, 'I just tell it like it is.' And the VP says, 'Don't give me that crap. You're rude and arrogant and it's gotta stop.' And because he respects the guy, it sinks in."

GM interrupts. "You're all very imaginative! But you're sharing an unwarranted assumption. You're assuming that this young man will only change if somebody talks to him. Granted, that *is* the way we're often made aware of our shortcomings, but in a case like this, in which the person doesn't listen to criticism very well, isn't there any way he can be changed through the story itself?"

We look at him blankly. "What do you mean?"

"Sometimes we're changed by the things we experience," he says, "and only in retrospect do we realize what happened."

He turns to the new homeowner. "In your case, you became interested in insects because of a new and unexpected storyline: 'The Mystery of the Holes in the Deck.' Only afterwards did you realize what had happened."

He turns to the couple that said their outlook on their relationship had changed when they became parents. "You two changed from focusing on each other to focusing on your son because of a new storyline entitled,

'The Stork Pays a Visit.' But the change wasn't entirely deliberate on your part. The new situation challenged you to change your behavior."

He turns back to the entire group. "Being the imaginative folks that you are, can you think of storylines that could help this young man we've been talking about?"

"Wow," somebody says, "you want us to think like novelists."

"That's right," he replies. "Good novelists don't preach. They get their heroes and heroines to change by putting them through storylines that will cause them to do so. That's one of the talents novelists have: the ability to transform their characters by means of the plot."

We all look at each other. "Are there any novelists in the house?"

GM is amused. "Doesn't anyone want to try?"

"I think it's a trick question," I tell him.

"Why do you say that?"

"Because I've been paying attention. You've made it clear that he's the way he is because of all the stories he's lived through so far. A moment ago you added that, if he's going to change, it's going to be through new storylines. And now you just admitted that you're thinking on the level of a novelist, not a short story writer."

"So?"

"So… if this guy's going to change, it's not going to happen overnight."

"Granted."

"But it's also not going to happen over the next week. At bare minimum, it'll take months; more likely, years."

GM nods. "Probably the rest of his life, I would think."

"Ah-*ha!* You admit it! That means it'll be a series of storylines spanning many years."

"Probably so."

"I would even guess that it would be a number of *different* storylines covering a *variety* of aspects of his life. Both personal and professional relationships would most likely be involved. The web of interrelated stories would be so big and complex that even the most intricate novel would be simplistic by comparison."

"I would agree with you," he says.

"We may be able to hint at some of these storylines," I say. "Maybe he falls in love, maybe he's affected by his relationships with the disadvantaged, maybe his supervisor exerts some influence on him—but these are only guesses, and they're merely pieces of the puzzle. A real-life transformation would be a massive intertwining of diverse storylines causing the young man to evolve so slowly and subtly that he himself barely notices it happening."

"Again, I agree," he says.

"So..." I continue, "we couldn't possibly spell out all the storylines that would be needed to bring about such a transformation. It would be beyond the mental capacity of any human to do that. I mean... we'd have to be—"

"God?" he says.

He and I look at each other a moment, then we both laugh. He turns to the rest of the group. "*Now* we're ready to talk about what God does from 9 to 5."

8 WHAT GOD DOES

"Does everyone remember our magical observation booth?" GM asks.

"Of course," we reply. "That's where we can see everything happening in the city all at once. And we can also hear what people are thinking and feel what they're feeling."

"Right," he says. "I used that analogy earlier to argue that God's observation of us isn't passive. God recognizes problems, understands their causes, identifies relationships, and so on. But let's think again about this magical observation booth, now that we've talked so much about the complexity of our lives as individuals. Given everything I've said so far about the intricate web of subplots that make up our individual life histories, what advantage would there be for us individually if we could step into this observation booth?"

"That's obvious. You've been arguing that we don't really know ourselves, because there's too much to pay attention to. We're living through these stories, but there's so much going on, our intellects miss most of it. So if we could step into the magical observation booth, we'd see the whole picture. What we're only partially aware of now, we'd view in its entirety in the observation booth."

"Why is it important to see things in their entirety?" he asks.

"Because otherwise we tend to lose the forest through the trees," we say. "We miss the real point of it all because we're so busy working on the details."

"Of course," he reminds us, "our observation booth doesn't exist. You and I will never get to see our lives in their entirety. When we do make an effort to stop and survey the landscape, the best we can do is gather up the fragments of memories gleaned from our own observations. And as I've already argued at length, our skills are incredibly meager compared to the wealth of information that's there to be observed."

"You're depressing me!" somebody says with a laugh. "You make me wonder why we even try."

"That's not my intention. We humans are actually pretty good at piecing our lives together in narrative form and using that information to set goals and make plans. I'm just emphasizing the vast difference between our attempts at this and God's ability to see it all. And the only reason I'm doing that is to answer the question that I've been asked tonight.

"That question is: 'What does God do from 9 to 5?' My strategy so far has been to get you to think about what *we* do from 9 to 5. On the surface, we play certain roles and perform work of some kind, in exchange for financial remuneration and a particular status in our society. But I've been trying to show you that we're doing much, much more than just working. We're each living out this vast story that I've been describing. We're gaining a wide array of competencies and evolving into unique individuals.

"It's in relation to us that the question has been asked, after all. We don't really care what God is doing from 9 to 5 on the planet Pluto or in the neighborhood of Alpha Centari. We want to know what God is doing in *our* lives. Isn't that what the question is really about?"

Savannah and I nod.

"So," he says, "I think there are several things that God does while we're earning our paychecks. The first thing I've already mentioned: *God actively observes us.* In other words, it isn't just a vacant stare. God is noticing all the interrelationships, tracing all the subplots. God is viewing our lives both in their entirety and in the greatest possible detail, getting both the big picture and the nitty gritty.

"Second: *God roots for us.* God really does want to see us become happy and productive. Unfortunately, God can't just make us that way. We have to grow into it. And we do that by successfully navigating the various subplots of our vast life histories. God watches these stories unfold and cheers for us as we experience them, but our happiness and fruitfulness depend on how we respond to the challenges that come our way.

"Third: *God tries to communicate with us.* Imagine that you're in the magical observation booth. You're watching the life history of someone you care about very deeply. She's developing certain habits that are making her miserable, and she doesn't even realize what she's doing. *You* see clearly what the problem is, but *she* doesn't have a clue. What do you do?"

Members of the group all talk at once. One way or another, we agree that we would try to get a message to her.

"But suppose you're *not* in a magical observation booth," GM says. "You're God. Which means you're invisible. And you can't just talk to people out loud—not as a general rule, anyway. So how can you get the message to her?"

"You can put the idea into her head," someone says. "Just an idea out of the blue."

"Or you can speak to her while she's sleeping, through her dreams," suggests someone else.

"And if she's not receptive to either of those options, you could rely upon someone who *is* receptive to you and ask them to talk to her on your behalf."

"Or here's another idea. You could have her turn on the TV just in time to see a news segment or a drama where someone is making exactly the mistake that she's making, and she can see what results from it."

"Or have her overhear a conversation where people are talking about somebody else who has the same problem."

"Or influence her to read a book or magazine article about it."

"These are all excellent suggestions," GM says. "You've got the idea. This is one of the things I believe God does all day. Using methods like these and perhaps many others, God tries to communicate with us and give us glimpses of how we look from God's vantage point.

"But let me emphasize that God's vantage point is radically different from ours. We can't see even our own individual life histories adequately. But God sees not only our entire life histories but also how our individual histories fit into the larger story of our society. In other words, God's view of us and of our situation far surpasses anything we can imagine. What God thinks of us is surely not what we think of ourselves—not even close.

> *For my thoughts are not your thoughts,*
> *neither are your ways my ways,*
> *says the Lord.*
> *For as the heavens are higher than the earth,*
> *so are my ways higher than your ways*
> *and my thoughts than your thoughts."*

"Isaiah 55:7-9," says NB.

GM continues. "This is why it's so important for us to cultivate a give-and-take relationship with God. If God can get through to us directly—through 'ideas out of the blue,' as someone said a moment ago—so much the better. But it's usually not that simple.

"So there's a fourth thing God does all day to try to reach us: *God influences the storylines of our individual histories.* Where direct communication fails, God works within the storylines themselves, not only to shape us into the people we're meant to be, but also to move us into social situations that are appropriate for us.

"The Bible gives us some dramatic examples of this. Consider the story of Joseph, who was sold into slavery by his brothers."

"Because of his Amazing Technicolor Dreamcoat," somebody says.

His neighbor smirks. "You've seen the musical. Now read The Book!"

"Everybody's got an angle in this story," GM says. "Joseph's brothers want to get rid of him. The slave traders want money for him. Potiphar wants good service from him. Potiphar's wife wants him for a plaything. Poor Joseph is a mere pawn in the game of life, tossed around the gameboard by others who have more power than he does.

"Or so it seems. By story's end, he becomes a governor in Egypt and saves his people from a great famine. It's instructive to look closely at the details of this story and notice how Joseph becomes victorious. Nobody's on his side. No one in power wishes him well or writes him a letter of recommendation. And yet the story moves powerfully and inexorably toward its conclusion. All the characters behave selfishly, yet their actions work together to bring about Joseph's rise to power.

"This story is a vivid illustration of the point I'm trying to make. When Joseph is sold into slavery, he's ill-equipped to become a governor in Egypt. The story itself molds him into the person he is supposed to be, and the contributions of all the other characters, although selfishly motivated, nonetheless move him into position. Everybody's actions all together bring about both the transformation of Joseph's personality and the circumstances necessary to elevate him.

"But I want you to notice what Joseph says when the story's over. He tells his brothers, 'You meant to do evil against me, but God meant it for good.'"

"Genesis 50:20," says NB.

"In other words, '*You* thought *you* were the ones bringing about this sequence of events, but you weren't—or at least not single-handedly. Your actions contributed, of course, and you're responsible for what you did, but those actions fit right into God's plan. You didn't know that, and you wouldn't have cared even if you did know it. You and God wanted the same thing, for different reasons. *You* just wanted to harm me, but

God wanted to use your actions to bring about a larger good.'

"I especially like the Hebrew word in this passage. The word translated 'meant' is *khawshab*. It means to 'intend' or 'mean to do' something, but it also means to 'plait' or 'braid' or 'interweave.' So Joseph is saying, '*You* were trying to do evil, but God weaved your actions into something good.'

"This is what I suggest that God does all the time, everywhere, in the life of anyone who is receptive to such interweaving. God takes the whole of our experience—all the different subplots of our lives—and weaves these elements together to transform us into the people we're called to be."

I interrupt. "But what does this have to do with our jobs?"

"Everything," he says. "Joseph's job is what the story's all about. God doesn't just want him to be religious or morally upright. God wants him to be an effective governor."

"And that's an important job," I admit, "especially since his mission is to prevent people from starving. But I'm an accountant. Although I like what I do, I wouldn't place it on the same level of importance as what Joseph did."

GM agrees. "I'm holding up the Joseph story as an illustration of the process. God weaves together all the subplots of our lives to transform us into His people—people who are not only religious and morally upright but also useful. To the extent that our jobs aid in that transformation, they're means to an end. But they're also important in their own right, because they give us opportunities to serve the larger world."

"Let's fast-forward to tomorrow morning," I suggest. "I'm balancing the general ledger. What difference does it make that God is weaving the subplots of my life, trying to make the stories come out right? I'm sitting there thinking, 'I can't get this account to balance.' What's that got to do with the story of my life?"

"You talk about balancing the general ledger as if it were an isolated task," he says. "It isn't. It's part of a story—actually, part of several stories. You can view it as part of the story of your day, for example. If someone asks you tomorrow evening, 'How was your day?' you might reply, 'Well, it was fine once I got that blankety-blank account to balance. It took me all morning and half the afternoon to find the problem. It turns out Monica forgot to key in her totals for the thirteenth. That's the third month in a row that she's messed up my figures. I'll have to talk to my boss about her.'

"So this is part of the story of your day. But (if you play along with my scenario) it's also part of the story of your ongoing relationship with Monica. It's part of the story of your department, especially the evolution of relationships and patterns of cooperation within your department.

"But perhaps more to the point, it's an episode in the evolution of the general ledger. You refer to this story yourself when your supervisor asks you about a particular line item. 'Why did expenses go up last month under this heading?' she asks. And you reply by telling the relevant part of the story—you explain the unique factors that caused increased expenses in that part of the company's operation. This may even prompt further discussion about whether last month was unusual or whether this is the beginning of a pattern that needs to be addressed. This is a subplot of the story of your own life, as well as a subplot of the story of your company's life. And if you think this subplot is irrelevant in the overall story of your own development or that of your company, I disagree. As I've tried to show tonight, we are who we are because of *all* the subplots that we've experienced—even seemingly minor ones like this. At any rate, there's more going on here than just the task at hand. Can you see that?"

"Yes," I admit. "But I'm trying to relate this to what you were saying about Joseph and his brothers. I'm going about my business, trying to get my numbers to balance. That's what I 'mean' to do. And you're interpreting Joseph as saying, '*You* just want your figures to add up, but *God* wants...' *what*?"

"To form us into people who will serve others in His name," he replies. "Whether you're an accountant balancing the general ledger or a surgeon saving a life makes little difference. God is working through everyone to build a better world. In big or little ways, our jobs give us opportunities to make the world a better place."

"Now we're getting somewhere," I say. "You slipped that part in at the end, but it sounds like that's where your thought is really headed. I'd be willing to bet that this is your most heartfelt answer to the question. You believe that what God is doing from 9 to 5 is inviting us to minister to one another through our secular roles. Am I right?"

"Definitely," he says. "But that's not all that God is doing. As I mentioned earlier, we all have shortcomings that keep us from serving others as well as we otherwise could. So God weaves together the disparate storylines of our daily lives to try to get through to us, and to cause us to mature to the point where we can serve others better."

The woman who talked about becoming a manager speaks up. "That's what I was saying happened to me. When I first joined my company, I was only interested in my own career goals. My experiences as a manager made me start caring much more about the people who reported to me, and that changed my outlook."

"This can happen to any of us," GM says, "but the spiritual significance of it becomes much more apparent if we pray a lot. Refer back to what I said a moment ago. God is trying to communicate with us. Prayer opens up our side of the conversation. The more we talk to God about every aspect of our lives *and listen for answers*, the more apt we'll be to hear what God is saying to us about our jobs. Ultimately, yes, God wants to use us as instruments in this world. God wants to minister to others through us—not just in religious ways, but in all the secular details.

"Notice how Christ describes His mission. He says His mandate is to bring good news to the poor, to free the prisoners, to give sight to the blind, and so on."

"Luke 4:18-19," says NB.

Savannah speaks up. "There was a Christian Socialist on the bus the other day. He said that we weren't doing God's will unless we were fighting oppression."

GM disagrees. "It's never a good idea to say that God's will is *only* this or that, but we can say with confidence that fighting oppression is one of the things God does. That much is true. We must remember, however, that oppression comes in many forms, some of them quite small. A new employee who feels unwelcome is oppressed. A supervisor who's burned out is in a kind of prison. Christ has come to free all people from every kind of trap into which they've fallen, and as Christ's followers, we're called to join Him in that ongoing adventure.

"He commissions the twelve apostles to

> *Heal the sick, cleanse the lepers, raise the dead, cast out devils. Freely ye have received, freely give.*

"Matthew 10:8," says NB.

77

"His work becomes our work," says GM. "What *He* does from 9 to 5, He wants to do through *us*.

"So... when I say that God wants to minister to others through us—not just in religious ways, but in all the secular details—I mean that God wants us to heal those who are sick and tired of their lives, revive those who are dead on their feet, restore those who are being shunned, and free people from their inner demons."

Someone interrupts. "Who are these people? Our coworkers? Our customers? Vendors?"

"Yes, yes, and yes," he replies. "Anyone you happen to meet, in any capacity, either through your job or through the community. God is in the business of renewing the world, and we are God's agents."

"I'm not a psychiatrist," someone protests. "I don't know how to do what you're talking about."

"That's good," replies GM. "If you told me you did have the answers, I'd worry about you. There's no formula. Only God knows how to do these things in people's lives, for the reason that I've already given: God transforms people through the various subplots of their complex life stories. Our job is to offer ourselves in God's service and to respond to every opportunity we see to support or comfort or prod others, however small those opportunities might be. Ultimately, that's what God does from 9 to 5. And He does it through us."

9 TROUBLE 'ROUND THE WATER COOLER

The next morning at the office, Savannah and I tell Cameron how glad we are that we went to hear GM. "He introduced us to ideas we've never thought about before," we say. "And we've never been part of a group that was so alert and ready to discuss a serious topic."

I confess that GM's answer to our question makes a lot of sense to me. "It's certainly better than anything I've heard so far. In fact, it incorporates the best features of answers I've heard, but overcomes their liabilities."

I point to my computer. "Harley said the other day that all God does is try to save souls. The work we do here in the office doesn't matter to God. If we're *not* saved, God is trying to save us. If we *are* saved, God wants us to share our testimony with our co-workers. End of story.

"GM's answer acknowledges the importance of salvation but integrates it into all of our activities, no matter how secular they may be. According to GM, God is trying to save us in every possible meaning of the word. Even if we've been Christians for years, we're still lacking skills and abilities that can enrich our lives and make us a greater blessing to those around us. And God is trying to guide us in the direction of developing those skills.

"Not only that, but GM's answer acknowledges the importance of our work. God isn't just interested in saving our souls. God also wants to enlist our help in making the world a better place. And we can do that through our jobs as well as through the other social roles we play in life. Harley denies this."

"What about Paula?" Savannah asks. "She made some good points about ethics in her email."

"Yes, she did," I reply. "And GM's answer incorporates her idea, too. If God really is watching all the storylines of our lives and coaxing us to do the right thing in each episode along the way, then that of course includes ethics. God encourages us to be honest, kind, diligent, thoughtful of others, and so on. But it also goes *beyond* ethics. To 'do the right thing' on GM's scheme can also mean to create more efficient procedures or to learn new skills. Or it can mean to assert ourselves or fight for our rights. What 'the right thing' is depends on each storyline. It has to do with the fullest development of our abilities, for our own sake as well as for the sakes of those around us. It includes morality, but it also transcends it.

"We weren't satisfied with Phil's answer the other day, either, about practicing the presence. We told him that we suspect we can get more from our relationship with God than just meditating upon God as we do our work. I think you and I were groping for an answer that we couldn't quite put into words. I can do it now.

"According to GM, God is more than just a loving presence. Talking to God is like being in touch with someone in the magical observation booth. God offers a higher perspective. We've got our heads down, our noses to the grindstone, but God stands above us all, seeing how our efforts fit together. To be in touch with God here in the office means we can do more than just feel God's presence; we can also receive guidance that will challenge us to learn and grow—and we can do this in very secular ways."

Cameron is looking at her own computer. She chuckles. "Sounds like you two are GM's biggest fans right now. Have you logged onto the Water Cooler Club?" That's the chat group we learned about last night. Participants have a chance to continue the discussion in greater detail.

"Not yet," we say.

"Well, take a look. It's not pretty."

We log on and are amazed to discover a couple of scathing criticisms.

"It was a sub-standard performance," writes someone with the sign-on name "Sifter." "Far below what we've come to expect from GM. There were so many things wrong with his remarks, I can't list them all. I'll just have to mention the four things that bugged me the most.

"First, he was too focused on the individual. That's what's wrong with religion in America today. Everybody's interested in his or her own spiritual well-being, and let the world and its problems be damned. That's a common attitude, but it's unlike GM to succumb to it.

"Second, GM assured us that, as we go about our daily business, God is watching us and rooting for us. Well, doesn't that warm your heart... *not!* I don't need God holding my hand while I work. Incidentally, if I was Emily Elizabeth and Clifford was staring at me through the schoolhouse window, I'd say 'Bad dog! Go home!' and I'd draw the blinds!"

Savannah and I turn to Cameron. "Ouch! These people are brutal."

She laughs. "GM encourages them not to mince any words."

"They certainly don't."

We continue reading. "Third, GM tells us that God is trying to get our attention throughout the workday, offering insights into how we can do our jobs better. I can see it now:

"'Psst, don't forget to write that memo.'

"'Psst, time to do maintenance on that machine. The belt's about to crack.'

"'Psst, don't forget to change the coffee filter.'

"Sheesh! I'd rather be an atheist."

Savannah and I stare at each other.

"Fourth, if all else fails, GM says, we can take comfort in knowing that God is manipulating us. We may think we're doing something for reasons A, B, or C, but it will turn out later that we really did it because God wanted to bring about D. So God used us, in other words! Personally, I don't want to be used, least of all by a Cosmic Puppeteer. On this view, our own plans and dreams are futile. God will either use them to bring about His purposes or else He'll veto them. Fabulous! Leave me out of it."

We page down to the next entry. "Veblen4Me" has a different complaint.

"It seems to me that GM didn't speak to the real issue. There are at least two ways the question can be interpreted: (1) What is God doing in our individual lives while we're working? or (2) What is God's role in the world of work? The first question is a lot easier than the second, but the second is more significant. GM chose to answer the easier, less-significant one. He reported on the status of God's relation to us while we're working; he should have told us what God does to contribute to the work effort. When someone asks me, 'What do you do from 9 to 5?' they're asking me how I contribute to society. How does God contribute? That's the question.

GM had an opportunity to give us another one of those massive, sweeping visions for which he's so well-known, but this time he tripped up."

We ask Cameron, "Does GM read these?"

"All the time. He says his favorite part of the Wednesday night discussion is Thursday morning. That's when he gets to find out what the group really thinks—especially after they've slept on it."

The other entries are much more positive. Many people say the objections are unfair. Others say they're too strongly worded but are important to consider.

"Does GM ever respond?"

"Yes, but he waits until people have had their say."

Savannah and I settle down to our work for the day. On my lunch break I post my own thoughts to the chat group, telling them what I think are the strengths of GM's answer. Later on, some other people agree.

Finally, Savannah voices her concern:

"Dr. Mane, I agree substantially with what you're saying, but so far what you've said has little to do with my job. I, too, believe that our work environment is a place to spread compassion and healing, because it puts us in contact with other people, but the work itself still sounds irrelevant. I thought you were going to tell us how God ministers to others *through our secular work*. You said a couple of times last night that 'God wants to minister to others through us—not just in religious ways, but in all the secular details.' That's what Dayton and I came to hear from you. Can you say more about what God does in the secular details?"

It isn't until Friday morning that GM posts a message.

"As always, thanks for sharing your honest reactions to our discussion. I must say, I feel sorry for poor Clifford. He's really not a bad dog, you know, although I suspect he *can* be a nuisance.

"Sifter, it's always fun to read your remarks. You and I have disagreed about a number of things over the years, but your criticisms have meant a lot to me. You have reminded me again and again that there is a thin line between insight and absurdity. As I strive constantly to walk that line, I know I can rely on you to help me keep my balance.

"It will come as no surprise to you, however, that I disagree with you. Let's begin with your third complaint, because that's where the real misunderstanding lies. You claim that I envision God nagging us, reminding us to change the coffee filter or to write a memo we've been putting off. Although amusing, this description reveals that I did not communicate my meaning clearly enough. God isn't trying to tell us things we already know. God is trying to convey to us ideas we have never yet imagined.

"To say that there is a God—at least for the Christian community—is to say that there is a Person whose love and intelligence and power are vastly beyond ours. When we speak of there being a God, we are saying something quite incredible. We're not merely saying that there's someone who loves us like our father and mother love us; we're saying that their love is, at best, a reflection of a far greater love. We're not merely saying that there's someone as smart as Einstein; we're saying that there's someone whose intelligence is unlike anything we've ever experienced. We're not saying that there's someone as powerful as a world statesman; we're saying that there's a power unlike anything a human being can ever display.

"Even the analogy I'm about to use is too simplistic, but perhaps it will help me convey this idea. Imagine that our magical observation booth does exist. And suppose that, just by standing inside it, our minds are expanded so that we can see and hear everything that is happening for a few miles' radius around the center of our city, all at once. We no longer have to shift attention from this person to that one but can focus on all of them simultaneously. A hundred thousand people may be talking at once, but we can hear them all. Nevertheless, we don't just see the whole; we still notice all the details no matter how small. Nor do we lose the historical context by focusing on the present. We recognize how this moment is part of the entire system of stories we were talking about the other night. We realize how these events happening now are episodes in the various subplots going on in the lives of all the people involved.

"The truth is, our brains aren't wired for this kind of work. We humans are supposedly able to multi-task under certain circumstances—or at least our managers say we can and must—but what I've just described goes way beyond multi-tasking. I'm not talking about doing two or three things at once. I'm talking about processing billions and billions of bits of information, both in detail and in general, both as things are happening and within the larger timeline.

"The magical observation booth has a small scope: just a few miles' radius around the center of our city. To say that there is a God is to claim that there's someone who does what I've just described, but does it everywhere and all the time, in megacities and small villages, wherever anything is happening at all, even at the bottom of the ocean and at the farthest reaches of space. Do you really believe that there is such a being? If anyone is tempted to say 'No,' I don't blame them. This is really quite a remarkable claim.

"But we're just getting started. To say that there is a God is not just to say that there is an Intelligence vastly beyond our own; it is also to say that this being *cares* about all this information. We're not saying that God is like a supercomputer, only more powerful. We're saying that God is personally invested in what's happening. Furthermore, this investment is goal-driven. God isn't just a passive information-processer. God evaluates what's happening according to God's own intelligence, which (I say at the risk of being redundant) is vastly beyond our own. In other words, God doesn't just know everything that has ever happened and everything that's happening now. God also knows things that we have never yet imagined—things so far beyond our experience as a species that we could not possibly imagine them. God knows better than we do how life could be lived on this earth: not just a little better, not even a lot better, but vastly better than we do.

"The good news of the gospel is that this same God is always trying to break through to us, always trying to convey to us the terms of a better life. The scriptures don't give us all the answers; they point us to the God who holds the answers. And God is whispering to us all the time, beckoning us to become the people we were created to become.

"But we don't become who God intended us to be in one quick transformation. As I explained the other night, we are who we are because of all the things we've said, done, and thought in all the subplots of our life stories. Everything we do every day makes us who we are. So God is constantly suggesting to us the kinds of detailed changes that could be made in every aspect of our lives, all of which—combined—could make us new people and could transform our social environments.

"No, Sifter, God isn't whispering to us to change the coffee filter. God is telling us that there are greater possibilities than we've ever dreamed of, right where we are, to make this a better world. If we heed this call, blessed are we, and blessed are those around us. For this is precisely how God's work is done on earth.

"It should be clear by now, Sifter, that your first objection was also based on a misunderstanding. I'm not preaching a message of individual salvation. I'm proclaiming a God who wants to transform the world, but who does so by reaching individuals. It's a social gospel, but it's brought about through people.

"You said in your second objection that you don't need God to hold your hand. In one sense, that's commendable. We Christians often talk like weaklings. Those who don't share our faith shake their heads in dismay when they hear us say, 'Of mine own strength I can do nothing.' They don't want to become like us because we sound like we can't even get through the day without divine assistance.

"But that isn't what we Christians mean. What we're trying to say, however falteringly, is that we're aiming to do far more than 'get through the day.' We have our sights set on this vastly superior being whom I described a moment ago, and we want to be like Him. *Of course* people can get through the day without Jesus! The world is full of people doing it all the time. But because we've encountered Him personally and have caught a glimpse of who He is, we're no longer content to just 'get through the day.' We want to live supremely! We want to be children of the Most High! And *that* we cannot do without God's help.

"Finally, you worry about the possibility of being used by God, meaning that your words and actions would not be your own but merely the dictates of 'a

Cosmic Puppeteer.' This is not how we Christians view our relationship with God. We want to be like Jesus. We want to think and act like He would think and act if He were in our place. But we also know how hard it is for us to understand God's intentions for us, so we strive for the next best thing: we hope that God will work through us and bring about His intentions for us in the ongoing subplots of our life histories. In other words, we hope that God will shape us through the events of our lives even when we don't recognize how we're being shaped. We're willing to submit to this shaping process because we want most of all to become like Jesus, even if we don't always understand how the process works. It isn't manipulation. It's yielding ourselves to Someone whom we trust implicitly, Someone who has our best interests at heart.

"Okay… I'll stop beating up on Sifter for today. There are two other people whose remarks deserve special notice. And I promise not to beat up on them.

"Veblen, I confess. I saw as well as you did that there were two directions I could go with the conversation the other night, and I did indeed choose the easier of the two. I hoped that no one would notice. I should have known better.

"But I went in that direction for two very good reasons. First, I do believe, as I mentioned to Sifter a moment ago, that although God's *agenda* is social, God's *method* is to work through individuals. So we really did need to begin talking about this subject at the individual level the other night. I confess, though, that I was hoping we wouldn't have to continue, which brings me to my second reason: I'm not confident that I can do a good job of answering this question on the social level. It was hard enough describing the complexity of the individual's life history; imagine trying to describe God's involvement in the social world! I shrink from the task. But you're quite right, Veblen. If I don't at least try to tackle this larger issue then I'll be failing to address the real nub of the question. I'll do my best next Wednesday night, if the rest of the group is willing. Just remember: I warned you. I may do nothing more than embarrass myself. But I will try.

"And finally, my apologies to Savannah. I think I'm beginning to understand what you and Dayton had in mind when you posed your question the other night. It sounds like you're looking for vivid examples of what God does in the work world. The heroes of Christian faith are mostly people who lived long ago, in faraway lands. The average person lacks the imagination to see how God is working in our lives here and now, under modern conditions and through today's technology. And because we don't have contemporary stories to guide us, we either turn back to the old, old stories and try to relive those adventures in our own time, outside their proper context, or else we settle for humdrum lives, unable to recognize how our own experience fits into God's ongoing adventure in the world.

"I believe that God's adventure is still going on all around us and that we're called to participate in that adventure *on the job*. I'll do my best to provide concrete examples of that idea before we're finished.

"Well, everyone, we've got our work cut out for us. See you next week!"

10 STARTING OVER

It's Wednesday night, and most of the same people are back again. We're mingling and waiting for GM. Savannah and I are talking to a distinguished-looking gentleman named Max.

"Oh, yes, this happens all the time," he tells us. "The Water Cooler Club rarely lets a subject rest after one night. We like to see GM keep trying until he gets it right."

We laugh, and he chuckles slightly. After a moment's hesitation, Savannah says, "You weren't joking, were you?"

"Not entirely. It isn't that GM's initial answers are wrong; they just aren't enough. To use a musical metaphor, I think of him as a composer of symphonies. He doesn't write quintets. He can't give us his best work in a sonata or an overture. His vision is so panoramic, it requires a larger format. It usually takes him two or three evenings to get his ideas across to us. But once we catch the vision, it's breathtaking."

He grows reflective a moment. "GM and I once had a conversation about this. Very early in his ministry, his theology was more simplistic. He was quite willing to condense God's mind and will to a fifteen-minute sermon. Then one day he saw a book sitting out on a table and it caught his eye. The title alone brought him up short. It was called, *Your God Is Too Small.*"

NB passes nearby and says, "JB Phillips. London, Epworth Press, 1952. Multiple reprints."

"He said the book itself made many good points, but the title has always stayed with him. Whenever he catches himself making definitive statements about the Divine Mind, he stops himself and says, 'Watch out! Your conception of God will *always* be smaller than God Himself. Never forget that.' That's been one of his main themes ever since: that there's far more to God than we can possibly conceptualize, even in our best moments.

"It's very important that you know this about GM: whatever question you ask him, his answer is not meant to be exhaustive. God may be doing any number of things from 9 to 5, but GM will tell you only some of those things—only the ones of which he himself is aware."

"Can anyone do better than that?" Savannah asks.

"No, but it's rare for philosophers to admit it. GM knows his limitations. He'd be extremely reluctant to share his ideas if he thought we'd interpret them as definitive answers. He's not trying to write a job description for God. He's simply telling us that part of the picture that he can see so far. And he hopes that that will be enough to get us started on our own explorations."

GM enters the room and we all find our places. After a brief invocation, he begins.

"We're still talking about what God does from 9 to 5. Tonight, however, we've been challenged to answer the question on a more abstract level: to explain what God does in the work world itself and not just in the lives of the people who are laboring within it. We must view ourselves all together as a totality, not as individuals but as a society of working people.

"I'm worried about this, because in our era we're readily familiar with macro-level thinking. We do it all the time, and we're quite unreflective about it. Precisely for this reason, we have a hard time seeing the work world as it really is. We confuse our abstract concept for the thing itself. My task is to open your eyes, so that you can see past what seems obvious.

"Here's my strategy. As we did last week, I suggest that we continue to stay focused on what it is *we're* doing from 9 to 5, in order to catch glimpses of what God is doing in our midst. I also want to continue to focus more than ever on what we're *doing* together. Let's pay attention to the *actions* that are being done, rather than the agents who are performing those actions.

What are we trying to *do* out in the work world? That's where I suggest that we begin."

"That's simple," somebody replies. "We're making money. That's the end-all and be-all: the Almighty Dollar. Everything else is secondary."

GM shakes his head. "Money is inextricably woven into the process, but I can't agree with you in giving it the primary place. You'll understand why, shortly."

"Let me see if I understand," says someone else. "You're asking us to think of the work world as a network of *activities* rather than name-brand entities. For example, instead of imagining the world of commerce in terms of *companies* like IBM and Exxon, you're inviting us to think in terms of *activities* like 'producing and distributing computers' or 'refining and distributing oil.' Is that right?"

"Yes," he says. "That's exactly what I'm asking you to do. Instead of picturing a hospital in your mind, I want you to think about 'healing sick and injured people.' Instead of envisioning Congress, I want you to imagine—"

"Doing nothing all day and getting paid for it?" somebody quips.

"—'making laws.' And so on. Do you follow me?"

We admit that we understand what he's saying... somewhat... but it's a strange way of going about it.

"It will all make sense later on," he assures us. "But let's dive down into one example and I'll show you where I'm going with all this. As I tell you this story, notice the activities within it.

"By the mid-1880s, many American cities became too large to provide for their citizens' most basic needs. Technology lagged behind demographics. Too many people were piled in too close together without adequate technological support. The story I'm about to tell concerns only one attempt to catch up. It's about the problem of milk.

"Fresh milk was hard to get in the cities. There were no cars or trucks to transport it from the farms; just horse-drawn wagons. And there weren't decent roads. By the time the wagons got to the cities, the milk would already be spoiled. This was bad, of course, because people need milk. Children do, especially. So how do we get milk to people?"

"What about canning it?" somebody suggests.

He nods. "Years before this story I'm going to tell you, the Borden Company began canning condensed milk. This was a breakthrough. It was now possible for milk to travel into the city from the farms, sit on a merchant's shelf, and still provide nourishment for families in the cities—especially for infants—without spoiling. But it also got some people thinking…

"Borden's condensed milk was sweetened. That was how they kept it from spoiling: by canning it in the same way that farmers canned peaches and pickles. Sugar was essential to the process. But this raised the question: Was it possible to can milk without having to sweeten it? Granted, city folk would still have to do without fresh

97

dairy milk, but could they at least have canned milk that didn't have sugar in it?

"John Meyenberg worked for a condensed milk company in Switzerland, and he thought a lot about this problem. His solution was something called evaporated milk: *unsweetened* condensed milk, in other words.

"He told his supervisors, but nobody cared. So he packed up his things and made the difficult journey to America, then inland to the German/Swiss settlement in St. Louis. Unfortunately, nobody in St. Louis cared, either.

"Meyenberg traveled east into Illinois, and eventually he came upon a small Swiss settlement that liked his idea. Several townspeople formed a Board of Directors, and the Helvetia Company was born. Later on, they adopted the name of their most famous product: the PET Milk Company."

The "Almighty Dollar" guy speaks up. "There, see? They liked his pitch and decided they could make some money. It's all about the money."

"It *is* about money," GM admits. "But they didn't just say, 'Let's make money.' They said, 'Let's make evaporated milk.' Granted, they thought it was a money-making proposition, but the only way they could ever get their hands on the money was to make and sell the product. Meyenberg presented them with a money-making *idea*, and *that's* where the story begins.

"There were the usual logistical problems at first. They had to find a building, and then they had to buy machinery and install it in that building. They had to set wages and establish policies and procedures, not only for their employees but also for the farmers who would supply the milk. They had to recruit workers—in manufacturing, sales, and distribution. They had to train all these people. These, of course, are the standard logistical problems that every business starting out has to address.

"Then the real problems began. The local bank collapsed, wiping out about a third of their funds. More money had to be raised in order to keep the company going. They got the plant up and running, but then it had to be shut down for process modifications. They got it back in operation and the sterilizer exploded, forcing them to close the plant again. Once that was replaced, they discovered that their water supply was insufficient. They tapped into existing wells in the community, but that still wasn't enough. New wells had to be dug. All of this happened within the first few months of the company's history.

"Now… I've asked you to focus on activities rather than on institutions or entities. Can you identify what's happening in this story?"

We think a moment, then various members of the group reply:

"A guy has an idea for a product…"

"He convinces other people to invest money and time into the idea…"

"They need a physical plant…"

"And machinery…"

"And workers…"

"In order to make the idea a reality, they've got to break it down into different responsibilities: producing the product, selling it, distributing it…"

"So lots of different *kinds* of workers are needed…"

"Don't forget support staff. Payroll people, for example…"

"And with all these workers, the founders have to make decisions about wages…"

"And company policies, including who's who in the chain of command…"

"But even all of that isn't enough. Major problems arise, and they have to overcome them."

GM says, "What you're describing is the beginning phases of a project. It's an ongoing goal that a bunch of people have agreed to pursue together. That goal is based on an idea: that they can produce unsweetened condensed milk, store it in a can, and sell it to mothers everywhere. Yes, they hope to make money. This isn't the kind of thing people do for a hobby. They've invested in it because they think it can earn them a profit—or at least the *owners* nurture that hope; the regular workers just want to earn a living. Money *is* a big motivation here; I'm not denying that. But in order to make money, all these people have agreed to pursue the goal of producing evaporated milk for the larger society, and that's why they're doing all the things you just described. They're devoting their time and energy—

and the founders are investing some of their money—toward the pursuit of that goal, because they believe in the basic idea: that evaporated milk is something the world ought to have."

Max's brows are knitted. "GM, why are you making this so hard?"

"What do you mean, Max?"

"The whole time you've been telling us this story, I've been imagining an alternative version—and it's the way most people would talk. In that other version, the protagonist would be the PET Milk Company. Once the company has been introduced into the narrative, any other storyteller would focus on that. They'd say, 'The PET Milk Company faced bankruptcy right in the beginning,' or, 'The company had to drill new wells because the ones in the surrounding community were insufficient.' The subject of the story would be the company. But you seem to be trying very hard to keep us focused on the people involved and the activities in which they're engaged. You're avoiding any mention of the corporation. Why?"

GM smiles. "Because the PET Milk Company never actually existed."

11 PHANTOMS

Max stares at GM. "What do you mean, the PET Milk Company never existed? I can show you history books that prove otherwise."

"I've read them," GM says. "But they don't prove what you think they do. They just tell the story differently."

"Yes—in a way that makes sense!"

"They use macro language that we intuitively understand," GM says. "But corporate entities like the PET Milk Company don't exist in the way that you and I exist. Or to phrase it differently, they have no independent existence apart from the people who work within them. We can point to their factories, but are those facilities what we have in mind when we talk about 'The Company'? We can visit their high-rise executive offices, but is that where 'The Company' resides?"

"Yes," we say.

"Really?" asks GM. "What happens if the office building burns down? Does 'The Company' cease to exist?"

"Well, no... but we do talk as if companies are spatially located. We say, 'They're headquartered in Omaha,' for example."

"Which means that that's where the corporate offices are located," says GM. "But the company itself doesn't reside there—or at least, not in the way that you reside at your home address."

Someone protests. "But you can go to the store and hold a can of PET Milk in your hand. Are you saying the can doesn't exist?"

GM laughs. "No, I'm not that kind of philosopher. Let me give you an example of what I'm saying. Imagine a marching band playing 'Rock Around the Clock.'"

"In the twenty-first century?" someone asks skeptically.

"Okay," GM says. "Imagine a 1950s marching band playing 'Rock Around the Clock.'"

"Better."

"There are one hundred high school students in this band. At the beginning of the song, they're in straight lines, vertically and horizontally; but all of a sudden seventy of the individuals fan out in all directions and form a circle. The remaining thirty stay in the center, ten of them forming an hour hand and twenty of them forming a minute hand."

"In other words, they get into a clock formation," somebody says.

"Exactly! But only for the duration of that song. When it's over, they leave that formation and go into another. Now... wouldn't it be silly if somebody in the audience were to say, 'Hey, where did the clock go?'"

"Of course," we reply. "Because there was never a real clock. There were just people temporarily creating a clock formation."

"And that's what a company is," says GM. "It's just people temporarily coming together for part of their day to engage in a common venture. For our own convenience, we refer to what we're *doing* as if it had independent existence; but that's just a kind of shorthand. When we talk about our company, we're actually referring to a complex web of interrelated activities that we all engage in as we pursue a common goal.

"Yes, we erect physical structures in which to perform these activities. Yes, we devise corporate logos which are visible on letterhead, billboards, and company vehicles. Yes, we may produce tangible goods that can be sold in stores. Yes, we register our company with the state so that it has certain legal rights and responsibilities. But these are all just physical artifacts pointing to something quite intangible: the shared activities that we've agreed to engage in, so that we can meet our common goals.

"There's a lot more to a corporate entity than just shared activities, of course. This web of interrelated activities implies a shared body of beliefs and commitments, a general willingness to obey designated authority figures within the group, and so on. It's much more complicated than I've been making it sound."

"Sounds pretty complicated to me," somebody says.

"But the important thing here is that our own activities make the company a reality, just like the members of the marching band make the clock temporarily real. Neither the company nor the clock exist without the people."

GM pauses, but no one seems ready to agree with him.

Max shakes his head. "I get what you're saying in principle, but our twenty-first century world is so deeply social, I just don't see the value of denying the reality of social groups."

GM nods. "That's the very reason why I hesitated to answer the question on this macro level: because the social world is, to us, as water is to aquatic creatures. We can barely even see the thing we're talking about. We're not only surrounded by it; we define ourselves in relation to it. It's woven into the fabric of our being.

"Let's extend the analogy I gave you a moment ago. Imagine a small town named Rockville. The residents want to do something extraordinary to put their town on the map. For one day during the tourist season, all able-bodied townspeople agree to take turns standing in clock formation on the town square, for twenty-four hours, and they actually move the hands of the clock to tell time accurately, accompanied by classic rock music. They call it, 'Rockville Around the Clock.'"

We groan.

"People divide up duties. Some build the needed props; others create music playlists and prepare to broadcast them over loudspeakers during the event. Uniforms are ordered, and all volunteers have to be fitted for them. Publicity must go out to state and regional media, to attract tourists. Refreshments must be provided and distributed to volunteers.

"Now... this is obviously much more elaborate than the clock formation of the marching band that we talked about a moment ago. Does *this* clock exist?"

"Of course not," we tell him.

"But it's very real to the citizens of Rockville," he says. "And it turns out to be such a success that they do it again next year, and the year after that and the year after that, until it becomes a local institution. Everybody in town talks about 'The Clock' as if it's an important part of their lives. They remember the year when Aunt Millie was finally too old and feeble to stand for her part in it. They talk about how Roger was at the tip of the minute hand and had only sixty seconds to propose to Faye, who was holding one of the numbers. The race is on to see which local family will be the first to have five generations participating in it. For the citizens of Rockville, 'The Clock' is very real."

"As an annual event," we reply, "but not as an actual clock."

"All right," he says. "Then what if the townspeople became very ambitious and decided to keep the clock going year-round? You say it's an annual event. What if they kept it going all the time? Would it be real then?"

"The time factor doesn't make any difference," we say. "They're just a bunch of people who are behaving like the pieces of a clock. The clock itself wouldn't become real even if they did it 24/7."

"But it's very real to them," GM says again.

"You're using the word 'real' in too different ways," someone says. "A 'real' clock is one that's either mechanical or electrical, and it's made of wood or plastic or some other material like that, with the express purpose of telling time. The Rockville Clock is not a real clock in that sense of the word. In fact, the charm of it is that it mimics a real clock. But when you say that 'The Clock' is 'real' to the citizens of Rockville, you mean something different: that the project has become important in their lives."

"Thanks for helping me drive home my point," GM says. "Corporations and other social groups are 'real' only in that second sense: as projects that are important in our lives."

People all over the parlor loudly object, but GM points to a young woman in the back. "Corporations and other groups do indeed exert an influence on our lives," she says, "so of course they're real to us in that sense.

But they're also real in the first sense, and I can prove it. In high school economics classes, the teacher will often assign a semester project in which the students have to create an imaginary business and go through the preliminary steps of setting it up. In other words, they simulate what it would be like to run a real business. Now... if we know the difference between an imaginary business and a real one, how can you say that businesses aren't real?"

A number of people around the room nod their heads approvingly.

GM nods too. "We know the difference between an imaginary business and a real one because a real one is registered with the state, handles real money, and so on, while an imaginary business for a high school project just simulates those steps. But that doesn't prove that a business is 'real' in the way that a clock is 'real,' because a business isn't a thing that's mechanical or electrical or made of a physical material like a clock is. I'm willing to admit that the world is full of real businesses, but I stand by my contention that businesses themselves have no independent reality apart from the individuals who work within them.

"Let's try another example. Marjorie and Ellie used to work in the same office, and they often had lunch together. When Ellie left to join another company, they stayed in touch, and they kept meeting for lunch. Year after year they've sent each other cards on their respective birthdays, and other things like that. They have a very real friendship—and by that I mean that their interest in each other has withstood the test of time, while some of their other friendships have come and gone. I admit that their friendship is real, but I wouldn't for a moment suggest that it's a real *thing*. We'd be crazy to say that a third thing now exists: Marjorie is one, Ellie is two, and their friendship is three.

"Or try this. Josie and Chad get married. Even though their relationship is legally recognized—it's as real as a marriage can be—that relationship itself is not a real *thing*. When we talk about them as 'a couple,' we aren't saying that there's some third thing: Josie, Chad, and their couplehood. We may refer to them as 'The Andersons,' but by that term we mean Josie and Chad.

"On the other hand, when they have a baby girl, we now count three existing things: Josie, Chad, and their daughter. 'The Anderson Family' is not a separate thing, but the baby is. The family is real, but it doesn't have an independent existence apart from the three members of which it is comprised."

Max shakes his head. "I still think you're making this harder than you need to. We all know that a friendship is nothing more than a relationship between two people, and a couple is, quite literally, two people who are in a relationship with each other. Everybody knows that the term 'family' denotes a group of people who live together and share a close genetic or legal bond to one another. Nobody would ever make the kinds of category mistakes that you're worried about."

"No indeed," GM agrees. "And yet we routinely make those kinds of mistakes when we talk about the world of work. Let's say that the Andersons start a family business. Chad is a plumber and Josie is the office manager. When their daughter grows up, she helps with the phones and the front desk. We know that we're just talking about the three of them when we speak of 'The Andersons,' but we forget all about that when we speak of 'Anderson Plumbing.' Suddenly we insist on thinking of the family business as a separate thing. And yet it's not. The term 'Anderson Plumbing' is just a shorthand way of referring to the ongoing project to which the members of the Anderson Family have committed a good part of their lives."

Someone interrupts. "But as you said a moment ago, a business has to be registered with the state. That makes it a separate thing."

GM shrugs. "Their marriage is registered with the state, too, but *that's* not a separate thing.

"For small businesses like Anderson Plumbing, we might not get confused. We might say, 'Chad's a great guy. He came right out to the house when I called,' or we might complain, 'Chad ripped me off. Look at this bill he sent me.' Because the service is provided by one person, we might not think of Chad's business as a separate thing. But if he extends his reach, hiring others to go into the field, perhaps even into neighboring towns, then it becomes much easier to talk about 'Anderson Plumbing' than to single out the owner. But when we do that, we're using a kind of shorthand. 'Anderson Plumbing' is a name we use in order to talk about the services that Chad and his employees provide."

Max nods. "I hear what you're saying, GM. We're all participants in various social groups, but the groups themselves are not separate things apart from us, even though our language makes it sound as if we think they are. My wife and I may talk about our marriage, but we're simply referring to how the two of us relate to each other, and we both know that. When our kids are visiting from out of town, one of them may mention 'our family,' but we all know we're just talking about ourselves and not something besides us.

"But I also hear you admitting that we *have* to treat corporate entities as if they were things, or else our conversations would be far too complicated. There are reasons why we resort to such language, especially when we're talking about the kinds of complex activities performed by businesses. If we didn't, then we'd get so bogged down in detailed descriptions that we'd never be able to communicate our thoughts. A simple sentence like 'Anderson Plumbing is fast and dependable,' would become so complicated, we'd never get to the point. We'd have to say, 'Out of the eight plumbers who work for Chad Anderson, five are fast and seven are dependable.' What started out as an endorsement would become so qualified, the original meaning would be lost."

GM laughs. "Yes, the truth is far more complex than we're usually prepared to acknowledge in daily discourse."

Max continues. "So if this shorthand is something we have to do—if we refer to corporate entities as if they have independent existence because the alternative would be too complicated—then why are you taking such pains to show us that it's not the truth?"

"Because we're trying to understand what God is doing in the work world," GM replies. "And although it's permissible—and even necessary, as you say—for us to speak of the work world as a thing, it is precisely that way of categorizing the subject that blocks us from seeing what God is doing from 9 to 5."

He turns to all of us. "As we proceed with this discussion, I ask you to join me in making this mental effort: even if we do accidentally resort to shorthand language and speak of corporate entities, let's not forget that we're actually talking about people joined together in a common pursuit. For example, instead of treating the PET Milk Company as a *thing*, let's constantly remind ourselves that we're talking about 'lots and lots of people cooperating to produce evaporated milk.' It's very important that we not lose sight of the difference. Promise?"

We all look around at each other and shrug. "If you say so."

"Now then," he continues, "the next step is to think of all this activity from a narrative perspective. Last week I said that, as we go through our days, each of us is playing out a complex life story—a vast web of interrelated subplots—and that we are who we are because of all of the things we've said and done and thought, within all those subplots."

"Right," someone says. "And it's open-ended. As long as we're still breathing, there's hope for us, because there are more subplots ahead, and it's possible that, going forward, we could make better choices than we've made before. That's what impressed me most about our discussion last week."

"That struck a chord with me, too," says someone else. "I've been doing a lot of thinking about it. No matter how old we are, we can change our course if we choose to do so. But it doesn't happen overnight. We play it out day by day, as the story unfolds."

"I'm glad you found that idea helpful," GM says. "Tonight I'm asking you to adjust the lens. Now I want you to zoom out from individuals and focus on our life *as a people*. Who we are *as a people* is the result of all the things we've said, thought, and done *together* in the even more complex story of '*us.*' That's what we need to talk about next."

12 THE COMPLEX STORY OF 'US'

GM ponders his next step. "I was going to return to the PET Milk example," he says, "but instead I'll try a different approach. Let's step back into our magical observation booth. From this vantage point, remember, we can see everything going on within a few miles' radius of the center of our city. This time, though, let's take advantage of the observation booth's historical capabilities. Imagine that we step inside and watch as the first settlers build homes in the area in the early 1800s. For mutual support, they draw up a city charter. As I keep emphasizing, some *thing* called 'The City' doesn't magically appear out of thin air the moment they agree to form a municipal unit. 'The City' is merely a mental construct based on the principles they agree upon and write down in their charter.

"At first we see moderate activity in the business district as the residents set up a variety of small-scale shops. Before long, however, newcomers with a lot of money build factories, and then the story picks up."

He points out a couple of imaginary spots in the air around him. "Here are the meat packers, down on the riverfront. Notice the increased riverboat traffic that results. See all the workers coming from the countryside and from other cities. Rows of tenement houses pop up to accommodate them.

"Several blocks away, a new company is established, grinding up the bones and gristle from the meat packers and making soap out of them. Rising above all this is the dome of the new city capitol building. The court house is two streets down, with the police and fire departments close by. A couple of newspapers compete for readers' attention."

"Isn't that 'The City,' magically appearing after all?" someone asks.

"These are visible signs of the 'The City,'" GM replies, "but 'The City' was already a legal entity before any of these physical structures were built. From the magical observation booth, we can see that it's the *people* who are doing all this—making agreements, then creating laws and engaging in enterprises within the legal framework of those agreements. Buildings are erected in order to perform their various activities, but the buildings themselves are merely physical manifestations of the projects to which these people are devoting their energies.

"The point is that people have come together to do

worthwhile things, and each new project opens opportunities for other projects. As these projects multiply, more and more people come into the picture, each one nourishing certain hopes and dreams, but also bringing their ideas and abilities. Because the observation booth allows us to see everything in context, we can pick out individuals and see that *this* and *this* and *this* one not only work for the same company but also worship together at the church down the street. Or we might note that *this* one and *that* one are politically conservative while this *other* one is liberal. The observation booth allows us to shift focus like a kaleidoscope. Each individual can be grouped with others in lots of different ways, but the groups, remember, don't have independent existence any more than the shapes within the kaleidoscope do. It's the people joining together that makes these groups real.

"Now let's focus on one project at a time. Which establishment shall we start with?"

"Since the meat packers aren't around in this town anymore," someone says, "let's start with the soap company."

"Fine!" GM says. "If we're in the magical observation booth and can watch the entire story of this soap company from its inception to the present time, what kinds of subplots will we see unfold?"

"Well," I say, "there's the storyline of its origin. Someone saw a need for the company to be formed and convinced others to join together in making it a reality."

"And that story alone can splinter off into other subplots," someone says: "how the company's founders got the idea for their product and developed a method for producing it; how they persisted until they found people who were willing to invest in the idea; how they made it all official legally by drawing up and signing the paperwork involved; how they divided up authority, not only among themselves but also how they created specific jobs and hired people to fill those jobs; how they solved all the problems that came up; and so on."

"What other plotlines can you think of?" GM asks.

"Once the people become organized and begin working together," someone says, "there's the story of their day-to-day cooperation. If the work flows smoothly, there may not seem to be much story material there, but it's still an unfolding story, isn't it?"

"One of great significance," GM says. "There are few things more wonderful than harmonious relations between people trying to accomplish worthwhile things. In practice, however, there are usually systemic breakdowns—processes that don't flow as smoothly as they're supposed to, or people who don't get along, or departments skirmishing over who's responsible for what. Those problems, and their solutions, are new subplots."

Someone else chimes in. "There's the story of how the public receives the product or service that the new organization offers—soap, in this case."

GM nods. "This subplot, too, can be quite complex,

as the public may not at first show much interest, and there may be a number of reasons why. Or there may be so much demand that the organization has to scramble to keep up. Or it may be that public demand is for something a bit different from the exact product or service that the organization currently offers, so the people in the organization have to rethink their original concept and adjust their work accordingly.

"And whenever we talk about the public's reaction to goods or services, we have to take into account competing organizations. Surely there were soap companies in other cities. How did our local company respond to that competition, and what was the outcome? That's a story in itself."

"What about changes in technology?" someone asks. "I'm willing to bet they don't make soap the way they used to."

"And I'll bet that's not the only technological change they've had to deal with," adds someone else. "There have been so many changes in technology since the company was founded, it's mind-boggling. Think of just the office equipment: typewriters, phones, air conditioning, copiers—"

"Organizations are constantly invited to consider big and small changes like these," GM says. "For each new type of technology, the decision process alone can be a circuitous story; but then the aftermath of each decision can also have ripple effects throughout the organization, sometimes for years to come."

"Don't forget my own field of accounting," I say. "It wasn't until after the soap company was formed that accounting methods became better defined, with distinctions made between financial accounting, capital accounting, and cost accounting. So the soap company surely had to adjust to those changes."

Savannah rolls her eyes. "Don't get him started!"

"Advertising!" says somebody else. "Magazine ads used to make a big deal out of soap and other hygiene products."

"A very big deal," says GM. "The soap and advertising industries mutually influenced each other's histories. That in itself is a huge story, as advertising agents conceived of new ways to capture people's attention about the various soaps and detergents, and product specialists within the soap companies had their imaginations kindled by their own advertising.

"Here's another major plot-line: how an organization implements legal constraints, like federal regulation. Our soap company, for example, may have started out dumping waste into the river right along with the meat packers, but before long they had to answer to government inspectors. Compliance with local, state, and federal law is a complex subplot all on its own.

"Now..." GM continues, "these are just a few plot-lines that come to mind, and there are probably many more. While we're in the magical observation booth, our minds are expanded so that we can take them all in—and not in a bookish way, as if we had only read about them;

we're actually able to experience them all, as if we're right there with each of the participants, feeling what they're feeling and thinking what they're thinking.

"This means, of course, that all those storylines we just talked about are interwoven. They're all playing out simultaneously, all part of a single ongoing experience. The exercise we just did was artificial. We talked about particular storylines for our convenience. In reality, all those storylines are bits and pieces of the whole. And when we're in the magical observation booth, we experience the whole.

"Let's pretend that you and I work for the soap company. From day to day, we see our small piece of the puzzle, from the vantage point of the department in which we work and the job that we perform within that department. But when we step into the magical observation booth, we see the whole picture. We experience the entire story of all the people who have come before us and all those who are laboring together with us now. In that booth, we live through the whole story of what we've accomplished as a company.

"Imagine how frustrating it would be to step out of the observation booth and try to communicate to others what we had experienced. Unless we're extremely selective, we wouldn't even be able to speak, and we'd have to do so much summarizing, we'd feel like we were leaving out important parts.

"What if we took the company history off the shelf and started reading it? What do you suppose we'd think of it?"

"We'd probably be critical of it," someone says. "We'd say, 'That's not how it was!'"

"Or even if the facts were accurate," says someone else, "we'd probably feel like there was something missing. The book would seem academic compared to what we've lived through. The characters in it would seem lifeless. We'd want to shout, 'These were real people! They did important things in this place!'"

"What you're admitting," GM says, "is that our history books are approximate descriptions of past events. Even the best ones can give us only glimpses of the lives that were lived before us. The experience itself was far richer than even the most detailed history book can convey. There's something more to daily life than we can record in books—and we can understand that intuitively, even though we can't fill in the blanks with language.

"Once we've stepped inside the magical observation booth and turned our gaze upon our company, we recognize that who we are as a company is the result of the whole story—of all that has been said and done and hoped and dreamed by all the participants. And this is true even though none of them knows the whole story."

We're silent, but we nod.

"What I just said is true of every other corporate organization in town." He points randomly in the air. "This school has the peculiar character it has because of all that has happened here—because of all the students, teachers, and administrators who have devoted years of their lives to the learning and teaching that have gone on here. This hospital is the way it is because of all the doctors, nurses, technicians, and administrators who have contributed to its ongoing story, as well as all the patients who have passed through. This police department is the way it is because of all the men and women who have worn the badge—and given their lives in service. I could keep going on, but hopefully you get the idea.

"Now I'm asking you to zoom out one more level. Let's step back into the magical observation booth and take a wider view. Instead of observing ourselves as a company or a school or a hospital, let's view ourselves as a city. A moment ago, we imagined experiencing the whole story of the soap company through the lives of all its employees. Now we're watching the story of the city unfold, and we're right in the thick of it with all the people involved, feeling what they're feeling and thinking what they're thinking. My question to you is, 'Who are these people?'"

We look at him quizzically. "What do you mean?"

"When you were watching the unfolding story of the soap company, you were there with all the employees. If I had asked you to watch the school, you would have seen the lives of the students, teachers, and administrators. If you had focused on the hospital, you would've seen the doctors, nurses, technicians, patients, and so on. Now I'm asking you to watch the story of our city unfold. Whose lives will you watch now?"

We still hesitate.

"Let me put it this way," he says. "Do you know if anyone has ever written a history of this city?"

"Probably," I say, "although I'm sure it's not a bestseller."

"And who do you suppose is in the cast of characters?"

"Oh! My guess would be our past mayors, tax assessors, drain commissioners, and so on."

"Exactly," he says. "But if we were to step into the magical observation booth and see the real life of this city in all its wonder and complexity, *then* who would comprise the cast of characters?"

"All of us, I suppose."

"Right," he says. "This city is the way it is because of everything that has happened in all the social groups within its borders: all the companies, schools, hospitals, media outlets—in short, because of everything we've said and done and thought as a people here in this place. Yes, our elected officials are part of that story, too, but *only* a part. The whole story—the one we'd see from within the magical observation booth—is the story of everything we've done here together. Do you agree?"

We agree.

"And what's true of this city is true also of our state. For our own convenience, we often reduce 'history' to '*political* history': the story of a city or state becomes that of its political leaders, or of its laws. But cities and states have the peculiar character they have because of all the lives that have been lived within them, not just because of the people who have governed them or the laws that have been passed by them.

"Zoom out another level. Now we view ourselves as a nation. Hopefully I don't have to prove the next point: that who we are as a nation is more than just a procession of presidents, a list of Congressional acts, and a series of wars. Yes, I know: that's the impression we may get from reading history books. But even the writers of our textbooks have made an effort in recent decades to widen the scope and to recognize the importance of social history. As I've been trying to show you, though, it's impossible for any historical representation to give us more than glimpses of the story. The real story—the one we'd see from inside the magical observation booth—is simply too big for the human mind to fathom."

Someone objects. "But if we can see what you're saying, doesn't that mean we *can* fathom it? Or else, how would we even know what you're talking about?"

"To fathom the full story," he says, "would mean that we could see it in all its length and breadth and depth. We humans can't do that. But we can imagine what it would be like to do so, and we can readily admit that it's beyond our ability."

"So why are we talking about it?" someone else asks. "If we can't grasp it, why's it matter?"

"Because we've been asked to explain, at least in

outline form, what it is that God does from 9 to 5, and my contention is that God grasps the whole, even though we can't. My reason for emphasizing this point will become clear very soon.

"Onward, then! If we as a nation are who we are because of all that we've said and done and thought as a people within all the social groups comprising our society, then the same is true of all other nations. No nation is the way it is simply because of its political or legislative history. Every nation has the distinctive character it has because of all the stories that have been played out within its borders—because of all the subplots going on within all the social organizations within that nation."

He looks around at us to make sure we're with him, and then he continues. "And who we are *as a human race—*"

"Ah-*hah!*" says Max as he slaps his knee.

Everyone turns and looks at him.

"*Now* I get it!" he says. "I know how you're going to answer the question!"

13 DESTINATION, PLEASE

Max continues. "I've been sitting here asking myself, 'What's GM up to? Why is he being so deliberate about directing our attention away from institutions?' Then I realized...

"When we speak of the work world as something impersonal, then it's hard enough for us to see any connection between *ourselves* and the work world, so it's even more of a stretch to see where *God* fits in.

"But you've been asking us to view the work world as an extension of ourselves. It's not a thing apart from us; it's something we *do*. Of course, it's in the aggregate—things we do *together*—but it's still essentially our own activities, and therefore it retains its personal character even though it's the actions of billions of people.

"*That's* why you've spent so much time tonight trying to convince us that corporations have no existence apart from us: because you want us to view them as extensions of ourselves. If we do, then it's easier to see why they're vitally interesting to God.

"Because if we buy into the idea you talked about last week, that God is involved in all the stories of our individual lives and is working through them to mold us into who we were meant to be, then it's plausible that God is equally involved in all the stories of our lives *as a people* and is working through those stories to mold us, *as a people*, into what God wants us to be."

GM is amused. "If I had known you were going to finish the job for me, Max, I'd have gone out for coffee and left it in your capable hands."

"Wait," someone says. "What just happened?"

GM shrugs. "Max summarized my answer before I had a chance to reveal it to you."

"You mean your answer to the question, 'What does God do from 9 to 5 on the macro level'?"

"Yes."

"And that answer is…?"

"That God is transforming us into the people we're meant to be—into the *world* we're meant to be. In biblical language, God is working through us collectively to bring about the reign of God on earth:

> *Thy Kingdom come,*
> *Thy will be done on earth*
> *as it is in Heaven.*

127

"For us Christians, that's the end-goal toward which humanity's story is moving, and everything we do is supposed to contribute to that goal. There are differing views among Christians as to how and when that's going to happen in its fullness, but all interested parties seem to agree on this much: that God's reign has both a present and a future aspect—that God is present in the world to some extent now, and yet the full manifestation of God's rule awaits some climactic future moment.

"The question, 'What does God do from 9 to 5?' is really just a more detailed version of the question, 'What is God doing *now* to bring about the full realization of God's reign here on earth?' And my short answer is, 'God is working through the subplots of the stories of all our corporate entities to fill in all the details necessary for bringing about the Kingdom of God on earth.'

"After all, when we talk about the coming reign of God, we're usually short on details. We don't think about all the things that would have to fall into place in order for it to be a reality. Over the course of our past two sessions I've been telling you that God is working out the details—slowly and painstakingly—through all the storylines of our individual and corporate lives."

"Can you give us an example of how God is doing that in the corporate realm?" someone asks.

"Certainly! Here in America, one very important storyline is the passing of the Civil Rights Act of 1964, which made it illegal to discriminate against anyone in public accommodations on the basis of the color of their skin or their national origin. Suddenly, corporate organizations throughout the United States had to change the way they did business: both who they served and how they treated them. It would be impossible for any human historian to trace all the details, and yet it's a significant storyline that played out in all organizations, all across the land, and in doing so, moved us closer to the kind of people God wants us to be.

"Here's another important subplot: there were laws passed and court precedents set around equal employment in America. Just the story of how those laws were passed and the precedents were set is immense, but consider the even bigger story of their implementation in all corporate organizations, all across America. Winning these battles in court or in legislative bodies was only the beginning; the details had to be worked out in corporate organizations everywhere in this nation, as employers found ways to make room for women and minority candidates in the hiring process."

"So it's all about ethics, then?" I ask him, a bit disappointed. I'm thinking back to the online chat Savannah and I had with our friend Paula a couple of weeks ago. We had told her that we thought God's interests extended beyond ethics; that God was interested in our work for its own sake and not just for its moral ramifications. "When it's all said and done, are the things we do from 9 to 5 important just because of their ethical implications?"

"Not at all," says GM. "Those were just some

obvious storylines that illustrate how God is working right now to move us closer to being God's people here on earth. But who we're becoming as a people is the result of *all* the decisions we make in *all* the storylines we share as a people.

"Let me give you an example of a subplot that isn't obvious: the massive story of our quest for knowledge. While there are undoubtedly some moral themes that run through this story, the main plotlines are about the paths through which we collect and disseminate knowledge in our society. To a significant extent, we are who we are as a people because of all the things we've said and done in this area, as well as all the ideas we've considered and rejected.

"Let's take just one small piece of this story: the ongoing work of scientific discovery. We may imagine solitary researchers toiling away in isolation, but that's not how science has been done for at least the past century. Peter Galison's book, *How Experiments End*, does a nice job of describing how complicated the field has become socially."

"Chicago," NB adds. "University of Chicago Press, 1987."

"He gives a few case studies in his book, but I'm focusing especially on the discovery of weak neutral currents within the field of particle physics in the 1970s. His story has a complex cast of characters: both experimental and theoretical physicists; a multinational team in Europe competing with an American team (split between East and West Coast contingents). The Europeans and the Americans both have long chains of command within their groups, as well as a variety of experimental sub-teams pursuing different lines of argument. It's a very complex story involving lots of people all over the world, with memos flying back and forth within each organization, every step of the way. It's very much like a corporation—multiple corporations, actually—but their goal is the pursuit of knowledge.

"I find Galison's narration fascinating because he shows that scientific discovery is a complex process of group decision-making. The people involved have to decide when they've got enough data, as well as how to interpret it. Then they have to choose which hypothesis best supports the data. Finally, they have to agree on when and how to announce their findings."

"You're losing me," someone says. "What's this got to do with the Kingdom of God?"

"It's one little piece of the puzzle—one small episode in a very big story: how we as a people have gained knowledge of the material world. God doesn't just want us to be morally upright; God also wants us to grow in our knowledge of the truth, in every way we can. Ethics is bound up in this story all along the way, but apart from its ethical ramifications, the quest for knowledge is itself an important part of our maturation as a people—as a human race."

I tell him, "I'm interested in hearing how you think

God is—or at least *can* be—involved in such a story. You speak of God whispering to us, guiding us toward ideas we haven't yet considered. Are you saying that God can help scientists uncover the truth about the natural world?"

"I'm saying that God does *precisely* that," he replies. "If there's one general category of working people in this world who are committed, at least in principle, to discovering the truth no matter what—even if they have to give up their old ideas—it's our scientists."

A young intellectual laughs and shakes his head. "I'm afraid you're a bit naïve."

GM smiles companionably. "I *know* I am. We all are, compared to God. I'm not saying that scientists enjoy giving up their old hypotheses, or that they make major revisions on a routine basis. I'm merely saying that they're one segment of the workforce that is often forced to do so, as an occupational requirement."

He turns back to me. "Whenever that happens, God is at work, even if none of the participants recognize God's presence. There have been those along the way who have acknowledged God's role in their discoveries—Johannes Kepler, Isaac Newton, and Michael Faraday are three giants whose names come to mind—but that's not the point. The point is that Christ's followers should recognize the role that God plays in the discovery of truths about our world, and we should have a healthy respect for what our scientists do. The development of scientific methods and apparatus is an important part of

God's story. It's an important part of *our* story as we've been guided toward greater light and truth, and toward our destiny as a people."

"Other than science," someone says, "can you give us examples of storylines that may be moving us toward the Kingdom of God in secular ways?"

"Yes," he says. "The idea of professionalism has spread like leaven across our society, not only here in America but elsewhere. It's not entirely a good development, but I believe it has had an overall maturing effect on us as a human race."

"Professionalism?" someone asks skeptically.

"Yes. Around the end of the nineteenth century, people in different fields of endeavor began to think of themselves as professionals and to insist on practitioners getting a rigorous education, passing certain exams, obtaining licenses, and so on. I don't just mean doctors and lawyers, although those were two groups that led the way. I'm also talking about social workers, teachers, and journalists, followed by business people, police officers, and so on; so that now, in the twenty-first century, we expect everyone, in any job whatsoever, to behave in a professional manner.

"Now, there are certainly moral and ethical constraints that go along with that. When we reprimand someone for acting in an unprofessional manner, we usually mean that he or she did something morally offensive. But ethics is only one small part of professionalism. As people in all lines of work strive to be more 'professional,' they subscribe to a complex set of beliefs and practices that are shared by others in that same line of work. They follow a set of standards, in other words, and they strive to attain and then practice a number of competencies. Aside from the ethical aspect of all this, there's something good about our striving for excellence in our work—striving to do what we do *well*. I believe that God is at work wherever people are committed to such an ideal."

He turns to me again. "But even though it's not merely about ethics, I don't want to downplay that side of it, either. Ethical considerations are woven into all our corporate storylines, in very subtle ways. The ideal of professionalism is Kingdom-like in several respects: it sets a standard of kindness that must be maintained regardless of how poorly our customers treat us; it's all about serving others rather than being served; it requires us to take ownership of problems as they come up and to work to get them resolved; it's about being an advocate for our customers and fighting for their rights.

"The more professional we try to be as a people, the closer we come to being Christ-like, at least in the ways I just mentioned. And society progresses by that much."

"Oh, GM!" cries a matronly woman near the front of the room. "How could you!"

"What's wrong, Madeline?"

"You're talking like a child of the Enlightenment!"

GM feigns a look of horror. "Heavens, no!"

We all laugh.

"Well, you are," she tells him. "You speak almost gleefully about the onward march of science, and how the professional ideal is improving us as a people. If I didn't know better, I'd think you believed in 'The Perfectibility of Man' and 'The Idea of Progress.'"

GM turns to all of us. "Let me explain Madeline's objection before I answer her. From the eighteenth century until the early twentieth, it was fashionable for thinking people to believe that the human race was on an upward course. They used the machine metaphor a lot. William Harvey showed that the human circulatory system worked like a machine and Isaac Newton said the solar system did, too. Adam Smith identified mechanisms that kept the economy running. It wasn't long before people claimed that even human history had a mechanistic character: that there were certain automatic processes at work behind the scenes, moving kings and parliaments like so many cogs and wheels.

"The machine metaphor was attractive for a lot of reasons, but perhaps the most important one was the belief that, if we could only understand how the machine worked, then we could get it to run better. If we could understand the economic and historical forces operating behind the scenes, then we could perfect society.

"Like all metaphors, this one partly illuminated the subject and partly obscured it. By the early twentieth century, both the idea of progress and of man's perfectibility fell out of favor among intellectuals."

"And well they should have!" says Madeline.

"I won't argue with you," he tells her. "Although I agree with many Enlightenment principles, I disagree with the Idea of Progress, for three reasons.

"First, the true history of the human race is not linear. It's a web of interconnected storylines so vast that no human being can fully comprehend it. The Idea of Progress assumed a linear view of history. Its proponents believed that we could trace our path upward from the jungle to the pinnacle of scientific achievement. As I've tried to show you, there's so much going on in our story at any time that it would be impossible to trace a single path within it. At best, we can say that we've made progress in certain storylines, relative to particular goals.

"Second, I don't believe that progress is inevitable. We make choices at every turn, and there are no guarantees that we'll make wise ones, even if we have the best information available to us. History illustrates this again and again, especially in our recent past. In a number of subplots we're regressing. The rich are getting richer and the poor poorer. Hatred and war are covering the earth like a dark cloud. Even though we know better, we're depleting the earth of its natural resources and making our planet uninhabitable for future generations. And all this is happening despite advances in both the physical and social sciences.

"Third, the Idea of Progress was simply about making improvements in our institutions, but the progress to which we Christians are committed is any move in the direction of the Kingdom of God on earth. Both the Idea of Progress and the Perfectibility of Man were secular versions of an older Christian aspiration: to become more like Jesus as a people. Sometimes those Enlightenment ideals have overlapped with Kingdom goals and sometimes they have not, but my commitment is to Christ and His coming Kingdom.

"Most of all, though, I want to emphasize the importance of choice in all this. In order to get this point across, I want to focus on a particular storyline. I'm tempted to say that it's the most important of them all."

14 POWER TRANSFERS

"It may be rash for me to say that any particular storyline is more important than the rest, but if there is one that fits that description, it may be this: the story of how power is distributed within an organization, and how it's wielded. The twentieth-century philosopher Bertrand Russell wrote a fascinating book about this."

NB adds, "*Power: A New Social Analysis*. New York, Norton Publishing, 1938."

"We work together in large corporate groups because it empowers us to do things we couldn't possibly accomplish alone. By banding together, we relinquish some of our freedom—we have to follow company protocol, for example, rather than doing *what*ever we want *when*ever we want—but we gain at least as much as we lose. Only some can lead and most must follow, but, as Russell points out in his book, that doesn't mean that the followers are no better than sheep; cooperation doesn't mean capitulation. Everyone benefits from cooperating; and we can list some of those benefits.

"First and most obviously, we benefit by creating a product or offering a service that would simply be impossible to accomplish on our own. By joining a corporate group, we become part of a team that does worthwhile things.

"But we benefit in a second, more subtle way: by having powers conferred upon us that we can't exercise apart from the group. In this society, only certain people have the authority to poke others with needles, to climb utility poles, or to arrest lawbreakers. If you want to do one of those things, you've got to get the proper certification and join a group that will authorize you to do them. You can't be a self-proclaimed nurse, telephone lineman, or police officer. You need to work for a medical practice or hospital, or the local phone company, or some level of law enforcement in order to exercise those kinds of powers.

"Every job offers this, although some do it more obviously than others. Every job authorizes us to do things that people outside that role cannot do. Some jobs give us access to privileged information. Others allow us to work with a wide range of special tools like expensive machinery, proprietary software, in-house manuals, or secret formulas. Of course, a measure of responsibility goes along with these perks, but right now I just want you to see that we have good reasons for working together with lots of other people; we are empowered by being part of something bigger than ourselves.

"But third, our roles within the organization allow us to express ourselves in ways we're not able to do otherwise. Each individual brings his or her own unique abilities into these roles. It's important for us to realize that each worker empowers the organization by sharing his or her expertise and personality with the group. In other words, power is being transferred back and forth constantly, from all to each and from each to all.

"We greatly oversimplify the situation when we assume that the top executives have all the power in an organization. *Everyone* has power. Some have more than others; but in everyone's case, including those in the top seats, the power comes from being linked with all the others. It's the joining together of all those people that gives the CEO his power. And although the CEO can make pronouncements, those words from on high will come to pass only if he wins cooperation from a significant number of people within the organization."

"So where are you going with this?" someone asks. "What's the storyline you want us to see here?"

GM replies, "As I said last week, God whispers and coaxes and beckons us—every one of us who will listen—to make the world better wherever we are. So if we view the workplace as an arena in which we all join together in various corporate groups—groups which simultaneously empower us and are empowered by us— then perhaps we can see that God is constantly influencing the big picture through every single individual who responds to God's overtures from day to day, from minute to minute."

Someone says, "In other words, this is just an illustration of how the way is being cleared, in the here and now, for the Kingdom of God?"

"Well, if that's your intention," says someone else, "then you've lost me. How is the way being cleared?"

"Through every choice we make on the job," GM says, "whether it's a policy decision or a case-by-case implementation, in everything we do and say, we're either helping to bring the human race closer to the objective or we're not. In that sense, there's an element of suspense in *all* the plot-lines of our corporate life. Every day, it's up to us to respond, and it remains to be seen whether we'll do so. But I'm also saying that this is a storyline in its own right—perhaps one of the most important of all the storylines within an organization: how competently the people within a company are increasing their power to do good and empowering others to do so, and how responsibly they're using the power they have.

"We talk about top-down *vs.* bottom-up companies, trickle-down *vs.* bubble-up communications within companies, centralization *vs.* decentralization, and so on. These are theoretical models. In real life, we're playing out our roles on a sliding scale somewhere between these sets of extremes. And within this context, God is whispering to each of us: encouraging us to work within our spheres of influence but also to increase our reach—

to expand our power base—in order to do even more good.

"This is one of the points that Bertrand Russell, who was no Christian, makes in his book: that it's a mistake for Christians to deny the desire for power, because it's perfectly in line with the Christian way of life to want to bless others and help them. The more power we have, the more we'll be able to do so. But he also argues that, because we're fallible humans who often don't recognize our own weaknesses, it's in everyone's best interest to distribute power broadly enough so that no one person or cadre of people has too much power. We shouldn't seek power at the expense of others; we should seek as much power as possible to do good, while insuring everyone else's right to exert power as well. I agree with Russell on this point. This is a theme that God is sounding again and again, in many different variations, to all listening ears."

"And I suppose," someone says, "this power you speak of can be entirely secular, involving quite technical issues that laymen might not even care about, right?"

"Right," says GM. "You'd have to be familiar with each particular field of endeavor to understand the issues involved. But God understands; and part of God's role from 9 to 5 is to encourage people to make good choices in such matters, and even to embolden them to do so when there's pressure to go in another direction.

"Let me give you a down-to-earth example of this.

Have you ever heard of the book, *Customer Service and the Imitation of Christ?*"

We have not.

"The author's name eludes me: Jim Jones... John Smith..."

"Ron Johnson," says NB.

"Same difference."

"But he's using his middle initial now. To make him stand out, you know."

"Oh," says GM. "That'll do it, I'm sure. Anyway, his book gives a number of examples of what I'm talking about. Customer service call centers tend to be highly regimented, top-down cultures. The employees who answer the phones have to follow a script, use the customer's name a specified number of times, look for opportunities to up-sell, and get the caller off the phone within so many minutes. They have to take their breaks exactly as scheduled. Rules like these govern their lives, and they're penalized if they don't obey. If you didn't know any better, you'd think they were quite powerless.

"But the author describes a kind of high-wire act he performs every day. He knows the rules and understands their importance, but his main focus is serving each customer in Jesus' name. He's very subtle in his approach. He insists that he's not advocating rebellion."

"Page 108," says NB.

"But he's clearly advocating a kind of vigilance that may sometimes put his readers at odds with their managers. He tells a story about how he got his company to make a sweeping policy change—"

"Pages 64-68," NB adds.

"—and that sounds very positive, but he skims over the fact that his supervisor opposed his efforts. It just so happened that she took a day off, and the manager covering for her gave him permission to move ahead on the project."

"Sounds sneaky," somebody says.

"He's really not that kind of guy," GM replies. "He felt it was providential. This was an important case, and he was sure that his company was in the wrong. By making a phone call, he was able to obtain documentation to prove his point, and he convinced his company to change the way they were doing business.

"Let me emphasize: he did not climb the corporate ladder as a result of this accomplishment. It's just one example of how a person on the bottom rung was able to influence his company, through prayer and persistence, and by exerting the little bit of power he had. His book is filled with examples of this tightrope walk—this balancing act between accepting the authority of those above him and wielding the power with which he's been entrusted."

A woman interrupts. "The health of any organization depends on our willingness to do that, doesn't it? If we all just obey, the group won't flourish."

"I agree," GM tells her. "As I said a moment ago, all corporate projects depend on a constant transfer of power from each to all and from all to each. That's what keeps them fresh and alive."

"GM," someone says, "you stuck your neck out earlier and claimed that this transfer of power may well be the most important of all storylines. Why did you say that?"

"Because everything hinges on the individuals within each organization. God's work is done at the corporate level only as individuals respond affirmatively to God's call and use the authority they have to lead their organizations in a Christ-like direction. That's why I spent so much time trying to show you that corporate entities have no independent existence. God doesn't work through corporate entities themselves; God works through individuals *within* those groups and encourages them to exert whatever power they have to influence the rest of the organization."

Savannah speaks up. "There was a man on the bus a couple of weeks ago—a Christian Socialist. He said that God has no interest in what we do from 9 to 5, because we're just slaves of the capitalist system. What God is doing, he said, is working to overthrow capitalism, not to help us do our jobs better. What you just finished saying seems like a plausible response to him."

"In what way?"

"I hope I'm not misinterpreting you. It sounds like you're saying that God *is* concerned about social justice, but that God works through us—as we do our jobs—to bring about a more humane world. The details are being worked out every day, through all the big and small issues we face in our office or factory. Every one of us is either helping to make our society more equitable or we're hindering it, but it's happening right where we are. God doesn't want us to stand aloof from it all and wait for some future revolution. We've got to roll up our sleeves and work for a better world right where we are."

GM nods. "I agree with you that God works through everything that's happening all the time, and influences people, both individually and collectively, to do what's right in each storyline, all along the way. In that sense, God's methods are evolutionary, not revolutionary.

"But I wouldn't dismiss that man on the bus too quickly, Savannah. For even though he doesn't seem to appreciate the positive roles that God is playing in the workplace right now, he does rightly understand that there's more to it than just participating in the Daily Grind. Let's pause for a moment to think about where this story of ours is headed."

15 THE END OF THE WORLD AS WE KNOW IT

"Just because I claim that God is involved in our daily work, please don't assume that that means God approves of our social and economic institutions as they stand. There are plenty of Christians who do assume that, of course. They believe that both our government and our economic system *as they are right now* were ordained by God. And because they believe that, they also believe that God is working to preserve these systems just the way they are. They agree with me that God is involved in what we do from 9 to 5, but their conception of God's involvement is static, not dynamic. Both politically and economically, they see God calling us to preserve the status quo.

"Now, there are some who believe God is calling us back to the way things used to be. They may differ among themselves as to how far back we're supposed to go. Some say we've got to return to the way we were before Franklin Roosevelt's New Deal was foisted on the American public. Others say we should go back even farther than that. At any rate, these people think that the story is heading in the wrong direction, and that God is trying to get us back to some former pristine state.

"But whether they're backward-looking or satisfied with the way things are right now, a lot of Christians seem to believe that God is primarily working to help us preserve what we have.

"I agree that our freedoms are always vulnerable, especially if we take them for granted. A lot of people sacrificed their lives and fortunes to secure these freedoms for us, and we must always be vigilant in safeguarding them for future generations. But I do not agree that God is merely trying to preserve our current political and economic institutions. God's focus has never been merely on keeping things the way they are. Throughout all of our history as a human race, God has been guiding us toward a greater destiny than anything we have yet accomplished as a people.

"I love this country," he says. "I'm deeply committed to the principles on which it was founded, and I've spent my life defending those principles by word and deed. But even in our best moments, neither this nation nor any nation lives up to the full promise of the coming Kingdom of God."

"Well, of course not!" someone says. "Until Christ returns and straightens things out, we human beings will have to muddle through. But under the circumstances, we're doing pretty good."

"I would say it this way," GM replies. "We're part of the massive saga of humanity's journey toward the reign of God on earth. We ourselves are living through current storylines within this saga, and—hopefully—we're playing our roles with integrity. But these storylines that we're living through right now are intertwined with the subplots of those who came before us and those who will come after us. We're all part of the ongoing struggle. At any moment in this story, we're always invited to come before God in a spirit of openness and confession; and if we do, then we'll be given opportunities to see just how far we've come... and the steps we're called to take from here.

"But it doesn't do us any good to pat ourselves on the back. When we assure ourselves that we're the greatest nation on earth, we sound an awful lot like our ancestors who built the Tower of Babel."

"Genesis 11:1-9," says NB.

"It wasn't just that they tried to create a structure reaching to the heavens. That project was merely one example of their overall attitude. They thought they were the greatest people on earth. The tower was just a symbol of their self-absorption. But before the job was finished, they became a divided people, scattered and confused. We should meditate soberly on the implications of that story.

"Any greatness we've achieved as a people has been

due to the One who has guided us this far. If there are any congratulations to be offered, they should be sent heavenward. By the same token, our Guide has never given us any reason to believe that we've reached our journey's end. Quite the contrary. God is always beckoning us forward and warning us against complacency."

"Come on, GM," someone says. "Even if we grant everything you say, I'd rather live in the US of A than anywhere else on earth."

"So would I," he admits. "But I'm also convinced that God has much greater plans for us than this, and is grieved at our inability to acknowledge how far we're falling short. Yes, we enjoy many freedoms in this land—or at least some of us do, depending on the color of our skin, our ethnic origin, our religion, our sexual orientation, or the size of our wallet. But we also tolerate great injustices every day, and as long as we ourselves aren't inconvenienced, we don't lose any sleep over it. We constantly tell ourselves that we're doing the best we can. But the story is headed toward a Day of Judgment, and we'll be part of it, whether we're prepared or not."

Josh, our token teenager, is enthusiastic. "Do you believe in the prophecies about the end of the world?"

GM's face is earnest. "I believe in a God who will not tolerate injustice indefinitely. Long... long... but not forever. Throughout each episode of our ongoing story, God beckons us and waits patiently, hoping we'll do the right thing. But whether we respond or not, God won't sit by and let it continue endlessly. As God heard the cries of the Israelites in Egypt and those of the slaves in America, so God hears the cries of the outcast and disadvantaged in our day. If we are God's people, we should tune our ears to hear what God hears—and take appropriate action."

"But the end of the world!" says Josh. "Do you believe in biblical prophecy about that?"

"Yes, Josh. Our scriptures teach that Christ will come again; that there will be a new heaven and a new earth, and that our tears will be wiped away."

"Revelation 20," NB says.

"I believe that. But it's much too convenient for us to cite end-time prophecies and wait for God to bring down the curtain. The scriptures also warn us that, when the end comes, we will have to answer for how we spent our days on earth *now*. 'I was suffering,' God will say, 'and you did nothing.'"

"Matthew 25:31-46," says NB.

"'I gave you resources,' God will say. 'What did you do with them?'"

"Same chapter, verses 14-30," NB says.

"Every storyline we're participating in now, both individually and collectively, is headed toward the coming Kingdom of God on earth. God is counting on every one of us *now*, using every means available to us, to 'proclaim liberty throughout all the land, unto all the inhabitants thereof.'"

"Leviticus 25:10," says NB, "King James Version.

Slightly out of context."

"Thanks for keeping me honest, NB. Yes, Christ will come. So our scriptures tell us. But His Spirit is also here… now… among us… and He's calling us to make this world a safer, saner place *today*, in His name."

Max interjects. "Just to clarify, GM: we're still speaking at the macro level, right? You're talking about what God is doing among us *as a people*, and not just individually—is that correct?"

"Yes, Max, although it's hard to disentangle the two when we talk about our responsibilities before God. If we *as a people* fail to respond to God's call, we're still responsible as individuals. We won't get off easy by saying, 'Isn't it a shame what our society is doing to African Americans or Hispanics or other minorities?' The question will be, 'What could you have done about it—not only at the voting booth but in your everyday life and in your daily work from 9 to 5?'

"We're individually responsible, Max, but yes— we're responsible for promoting God's purposes *within our social groups—including the companies we work for*. We can do very little as individuals. That's why we form corporations and other social groups, so that we can accomplish big things together.

"But, as Reinhold Niebuhr pointed out early in the twentieth century, you can take a bunch of morally-upright individuals and put them together into any sort of social group—a company, a government unit, or a nation—and you'll find them acting immorally *as a collective unit.*"

NB interrupts. "Reinhold Niebuhr, *Moral Man and Immoral Society: A Study in Ethics and Politics*. New York, Scribner's, 1932. Multiple reprints."

"No matter how ethical we may be as individuals, Niebuhr argued, we tend to behave unjustly when we work *together*. An obvious example of this is our seeming inability to establish and maintain peace on a global scale. Although the world is filled with individuals who want peace, nations are constantly at war with one another. Nor can we brush off this fact by blaming it on politicians. There are many reasons for the strife between nations, and they are not easily resolvable. Niebuhr's solution, like Bertrand Russell's, is to find ways to tame power in all its forms, both social and political; but, also like Russell, he's not terribly optimistic about that happening anytime soon. It's the ongoing story that will bring it about—a story to which all of us contribute every day.

"But bringing the matter closer to home, we often find young ministers, straight out of seminary, shaking their fists at multinational corporations and blaming them for inequities all around the world. But who *are* these corporations? Who are we blaming when we point in righteous indignation at the behavior of these corporations? We're probably thinking of the CEO, the CFO, the members of the board, and other highly-placed folks like that. But as I've been trying to show you tonight, a corporation is the way it is because of all the storylines that have played out within all the departments of that corporation. Everyone who works for a corporation is responsible for what that company does, at least to the extent of their authority within the company.

"Granted, that's the loophole; most employees would plead innocence because they don't sit in the top seats. But as I've been saying tonight, the people at the top have limited power. What power they have is derived from the complicity of thousands of employees. If a corporation is behaving immorally, then that means that thousands of employees are behaving immorally *together*, even though, as individuals, they may be wonderful human beings.

"This is what God is doing at the corporate level from 9 to 5: encouraging individuals within each company to behave as true people of God *within their roles* in those companies. I don't mean to reduce God's involvement to moral issues, however. God is calling everyone, in every department and at every level of authority, to lead their social groups forward—toward a better future for everyone."

Max speaks up again. "You know, GM, there's one obvious social group that most of us here belong to, and you haven't said a word about it. The *church* is a social group, after all."

"Yes it is," says GM. "And I've deliberately avoided saying anything about the church as an institution. Here's my reason: many Christians resist thinking about what God does from 9 to 5 because they assume that God works through the church *as an institution*, and therefore they, *as individuals*, are off the hook. They join the institution and contribute to it financially, and they leave it to the church *as an institution* to do the rest.

"But we are called to be the body of Christ in the world in every possible way. Granted, none of us can represent Christ adequately by ourselves. We do need organized religion. But Christ doesn't work through the church as an institution only; the 'body of Christ' is made manifest in the world as all of His followers go to their various stations and carry out their secular roles in His name. The 'body of Christ' is not an impersonal organization; it's *us*. It's all of us who profess His name and hear His voice, even though we interpret it in divergent ways. Through us—Protestant, Catholic, Anglican, Coptic, and Greek Orthodox—through all of us together, God is working to bring about a better world."

"What about people of other faiths?" a woman asks. "I have Muslim friends whose conduct would put many of us Christians to shame."

"I could say the same about some of my Jewish friends," adds someone else.

A third person asks, "Why stop at monotheists? Isn't God working through Hindus too?"

"And Buddhists?"

GM nods. "I've been describing God as a pervasive presence in all human affairs, vitally involved in

155

everything we're doing, all the time. I see no reason to limit God's activity merely to those of us who confess Jesus as the Christ. God is here for all of us, and wills to be a powerful influence for good in anyone's life, so long as we're the least bit receptive.

"Christ once told his disciples this very thing. Someone who was not a member of the church was healing people in Jesus' name, and the Apostle John told him he wasn't authorized to do so."

"Mark 9:38-50," says NB.

"But Jesus warned his disciples not to stand in the way of 'these little ones who believe in me.' The Greek word in this passage is not the one used for children; it's the word for 'the little people,' the ones who are overlooked or dismissed. Jesus says these 'little ones' are an important part of the team."

"Agreed, GM," says the woman with the Muslim friends, "but you sound a bit condescending. You speak as if we're the star players and those of other faiths are part of the bench."

"That was not my intention at all," he says. "We Christians naturally consider ourselves members of God's team. All I'm trying to point out is that God's team is bigger than we usually acknowledge. We're not the only ones on it.

"Next week I'll fulfill my promise to Savannah by inviting people to tell their stories. We'll hear concrete examples of how people have found God actively involved in their lives from 9 to 5. It might not be obvious as we're listening to those testimonies, so I'll point it out now: the doctrines of this or that church, or the creeds of this or that religion, play mostly a supporting role in our day-to-day lives. God works through all of us to the extent that we're receptive. We humans may be committed, more or less, to a certain body of beliefs about the world, about each other, and about God, but as I've said before, the real God is far, far beyond our feeble conceptions. None of us know God as He truly is. All of us have a lot to learn.

"But God doesn't let our faulty conceptions stand in the way of relating to us or working through us. Everyone is called to be on God's team. What He does from 9 to 5, He does through us—through every single person who will listen, even a little. God is working to make this world a better place for everyone, and is enlisting everyone's help to do so, every minute of every day.

"*That's* God's true work. *That's* what God does from 9 to 5."

16 DOES GOD MICROMANAGE OUR LIVES?

It's Thursday morning—Water Cooler Time—and I've risen an hour early to share my thoughts with the group.

"Dr. Mane," I write, "I was inspired by many of the things you said last night, and I especially appreciated the way you carefully laid it all out for us. When I left the meeting, I felt that I substantially agreed with you. I, too, believe in a God who is involved in the nitty-gritty and who deals with us both as individuals and as groups. But this morning there's something bothering me about your philosophy, and I've got to get it off my chest. It sounds to me as if, on your view, God micromanages our lives.

"Savannah and I were faced with this criticism ourselves a few weeks ago from a friend of ours. He said he could never believe in a God who always wants us to consult Him before we make any decision. 'God has put a good head on my shoulders,' he said, 'and He should trust me to make my own decisions.' When our friend said that to us, I didn't exactly understand what he meant, but as I listened to you last night his criticism became clearer, and it seemed quite pertinent.

"You say that God is vitally interested in everything we do, both as individuals and in concert with others. You also say that God interacts with us, whispering ideas to us and, when that fails, weaving the various subplots of our life histories together in a way that will cause us to grow, even if we don't always understand what's happening to us. On your view, God is very hands-on. But isn't that micromanaging? And if it is, shouldn't we be concerned about it?"

When I join Savannah on the bus an hour later, she's intrigued by the question. "I remember Carl challenging us on that point in his email a couple of weeks ago, but, to be honest, I haven't given it another thought."

"I haven't either," I tell her, "until last night. I started thinking ahead to the Water Cooler discussion, and I remembered Sifter's complaint about God being a Cosmic Puppeteer. And then I remembered what Carl said about God micromanaging. Once I started thinking about it, I didn't have a good answer for either Sifter or Carl. I'm interested in knowing what GM thinks."

During our lunchtime, we hide out in a corner of the cafeteria and read the responses together on our phones.

We're delighted to find a post from NB. "It occurs to

me," she says, "that the question, 'Does God micromanage?' depends, at least in part, on our answer to a prior question: 'Is a management model appropriate when we're talking about God?'"

Savannah interrupts. "Exactly! Remember how D portrayed God as the CEO of the planet? She assumed that that's what we thought, but we weren't quite satisfied with that view."

"Neither was she," I reply. "And she ended up rejecting belief in a Personal God simply because she assumed that a management model followed automatically from that. There's a lot riding on how we answer this question. We might end up not believing in God just because we've got a faulty view of how God might relate to us."

NB continues. "It might be helpful for me to provide some textual background, for the Bible does refer to God as a manager, or at least a case could be made that it does.

"In Genesis God puts Adam to work tilling the Garden of Eden (Gen 2:15) and gives humankind a supervisory role over all living things, presumably under God's supervision (Gen 1:26-30)."

Savannah turns to me again. "Remember how Harley insisted that work is a result of Adam and Eve's expulsion from the Garden of Eden? NB's got it right: God gave them work to do even while they were living in the Garden. Work wasn't a curse; it was a blessing. It became a curse only when it was divorced from everyday interaction with God."

We return to NB's remarks. "In the New Testament Gospels, Christ acts very much like a manager, delegating authority to his disciples and sending them out in his name: both the twelve (Matthew 10:1—11:1; Mark 3:13-15; Luke 9:1-6) and the seventy (Luke 10:1-20). He gives them errands just like a manager would (Matthew 21:1-3; 26:17-19). He speaks in parables that portray him as a manager over them (for example, the Parable of the Talents in Matthew 25:14-30 or of the Pounds in Luke 19:11-28; or the Parable of the Wicked Servant in Matthew 14:45-51 or the more general version in Mark 13:34-37). Just before he ascends to his Father he gives them a job to do and makes it clear that he's depending on them to keep doing his work (Matthew 28:16-20; Mark 16:15-16; Luke 24:44-49; Acts 1:3-8).

"All these passages picture God and/or Christ in a managerial role over us, and there are probably others that I haven't mentioned.

"But notice: in none of these cases does God micromanage. God puts Adam in charge of the Garden and lets him make a mess of things. Christ sends out the twelve and the seventy and waits for them to come back and give their report. The managers in the parables expect their servants to know what to do, and then the managers leave. Christ gives his disciples authority to continue his work in his absence. Whenever the Bible uses management imagery, the manager leaves and lets the servants do their own work.

"From a strictly textual point of view, then, I would have to say that God does not micromanage."

Someone who signed on as "BreathofGod" thanks NB for those comments but says there's more to the story. "The Bible uses many other images to describe God. What about the Holy Spirit? Do the scriptures ever describe the Holy Spirit as a manager?"

"Funny you should ask!" NB replies a little later. "As soon as the scriptures start talking about the work of the Holy Spirit in our lives, the metaphor changes. I may be missing some passages here, but it seems to me that the scriptures don't use the management metaphor when they talk about the work of the Spirit. Like I said in my earlier post, the biblical view of management seems to be hands-off, but the Holy Spirit works within us. So these are two very different metaphors, and when Christ and others talk about the Spirit, they don't mix the two metaphors.

"In short, the Holy Spirit isn't a manager. That's not an appropriate metaphor when we're talking about what the Spirit does in our lives.

"'I have been crucified with Christ,' Paul writes, 'and it is no longer I who live, but it is Christ who lives in me. And the life I now live in the flesh I live by faith in the Son of God, who loved me and gave himself for me' (Galatians 1:19-20).

"That's an incredibly intimate relationship. We're yielding our very selves to God, wishing for Christ to live through us. 'He must increase but I must decrease,' says John the Baptist (John 3:30).

"If we were to insist on a management model then this would be far worse than micromanaging, but I don't interpret this as a management model at all. This isn't some other person trying to get us to do things that he or she wants us to do. This is our Lord and our God dwelling within us, responding to our willingness to become children of God from the inside out. It's not a management model. It's an intertwining of ourselves with God, and it involves everything we think, say, and do.

"So here's how I would respond to BreathofGod's question:

"(1) When the Bible uses management imagery, it's merely to emphasize that we're accountable before God for the way we live, just as servants are accountable to their absent lord. The intention is to remind us that we'll have to answer to God someday even though God seems absent from this present world.

"But (2) God is not absent and therefore is not really a manager in that sense. God is ever-present and lives within us. We long to be one with God in everything we do. To the extent that we pray about our daily work, for example, we find the Spirit of God responding in ways that encourage us to be like Christ, even when we're engaged in secular tasks. But God isn't micromanaging at those moments because it's not a worker-manager relationship. It's a love story—one so deep it touches everything. We don't work *for* God in the way that we work for an earthly supervisor. We work *with* God to bring about God's will here on earth through us. And we can't possibly do that by our own power."

Savannah nods. "NB did a good job with that."

We skim over some other posts that applaud her for clarifying the subject, and then we read GM's response. He thanks NB for bringing a biblical perspective to the discussion, and he agrees with her contention that it's probably not appropriate to think of God as acting in a managerial capacity over us.

"But we must be careful not to side-step the main issue. For whether we use managerial language or not, Dayton has raised an objection that strikes at the heart of Christian faith, and if we can't answer it, then we should be deeply troubled.

"We Christians are faced with a dilemma whenever we talk about God's involvement in day-to-day life. On one hand, we want to say that every good experience is a blessing from God rather than the result of our own efforts; but on the other hand, we want to exonerate God from all the bad things that happen to us, and we point to human causation in such cases. **Does God determine our fate, or do we?** We can't have it both ways.

"Traditionally, we have maintained that God gives us free will. That means that God does not micromanage. But we have also insisted that 'all things work together for good for those who love God, who are called according to his purpose' (Romans 8:28). But if God somehow makes it all work out for the best, then that seems to imply that God does micromanage after all.

"The simplest way to handle this problem would be to deny that God is involved in our day-to-day lives. Throughout the centuries, and especially in our own time, there have been many well-meaning Christians who have taken this course. 'God gave me a brain and expects me to use it,' they say, and then they go about their lives as if there were not a God. They follow a moral code, they may even recite the Lord's Prayer, but they do not seek a personal relationship with God, and they become quite nettled with Christians who challenge them on this point. For them, Christianity is not about a relationship and, indeed, cannot be.

"While this solves the dilemma I just mentioned, it raises another one, for a relationship with God is what Christianity is all about, and if we deny that, then what's the point of being a Christian? Why not just live a good moral life and forget all about religion?

"Another alternative is to say that God does micromanage. In other words, it is God who determines what happens to us and not we ourselves. But this line of reasoning also denies historic Christian faith, for it deprives us of free will, and therefore of any responsibility for our actions.

"Obviously, any philosopher who wants to be faithful to Christian teaching will have to wrestle with Dayton's objection. The two easy solutions I just outlined are not historically viable options, although they've been tried many times by Christians over the centuries. There is no easy way out of this dilemma. Nevertheless, Dayton has challenged me to respond to it in an authentically Christian way.

"I have been urging you to consider life as a vast and complex web of intertwining stories. Who we are, both as individuals and as a people, is the result of all that we've said, done, and thought within this vast web of interrelated stories.

"If you'll think back to what I said about both the nature/nurture problem and The Idea of Progress, I do believe that we are who we are because of our own choices and not just because of the things that have happened to us. We are active participants in this vast web of stories. They are very much *our* stories, and they proceed on the basis of the choices we make. We're not puppets; we're active agents, and we're constantly making decisions that affect our destinies—both our own and the destinies of those around us.

"But here's where it gets complicated, because we're all in this together. *I* make choices, but so do *you*. *We* make choices, but so do lots and lots of other folks. Who we are as a people is the result of the things that *all of us* have said, done, and thought within this network of stories. Precisely for this reason, none of us can *control* our destinies. We can choose to go in certain directions or to become certain kinds of people, but we cannot control the outcome. No one can. Not even the most powerful individuals in the world can control the consequences of their choices; but all of us can and must make choices.

"In fact, what I've just said may be the hardest part of making decisions. If we knew beyond the shadow of a doubt what the outcome would be, most choices would be crystal clear. The hard part is deciding which way to go in the face of uncertain outcomes. This is a fact of life. The richest people on earth, or the ones with the greatest political power, are often frustrated right along with the poor and powerless. We all make choices, but no one can control how it all plays out.

"Dayton is asking me to declare myself relative to the obvious next question: Does *God* control the outcome? Is it God who decides what will happen, once we've made our choice and cast our lot?

"My answer is: No. God does not *control* our destinies. But somehow—and I must insist that you let me fall back on the limitations of the human mind here—somehow God is able to *influence* people—some more, some less—to respond to each day's events in ways that will make the world better for all of us. God is not controlling us; God is influencing us. And if we open ourselves to that influence, we can help make a better world.

"Now… I realize that this raises more questions than it answers, and there's not enough time to discuss them around the Water Cooler. We'll have to slate them for future Wednesday night sessions. But there is one more glaring question that I feel I must answer right now: If

God does not control our destinies, then on what basis can we hope for the ultimate triumph of good over evil?

"My answer is: Somehow, God's love can turn all our NOs into a YES.

"God's way is not and never has been to force people; and yet, it is precisely through people's evil choices that the love of God has been made manifest. We Christians insist that what Christ did on the cross was the most important part of his mission. But what does that mean? It means that God's plans were brought to fruition precisely by the evil choices of those who sought Christ's death. The triumph of God's will came about precisely through the apparent triumph of Christ's enemies. The power and love of God are often made visible at precisely those moments when the forces of evil seem to be overshadowing the forces of good. I don't know how that's possible. I only know that it's one of the cardinal principles of historic Christian faith.

"Does God micromanage? *No.*

"Does God control what happens to us? *No.*

"Can we trust God to work all things together for good? *Yes.*

"On what can we base this hope? *On the belief that the love of God is greater than any other power on earth, and God's love is somehow working through the subplots of our corporate life story, entreating all of us to do the things that will make this world better for everyone.*"

As Savannah and I walk back to our cubicles, she

grins at me. "Are you satisfied with his answer?"

"No," I admit. "But I realize there may not be an alternative. I keep thinking about what D told us: that she can't accept the view that God is in charge of the world. It sounds like GM would agree, up to a point. God isn't running things, according to GM, but God is right here in the trenches with us, working out the solutions *through* us, day by day, minute by minute."

"Is there really any other way?" Savannah asks. "Sometimes we talk as if we think God's going to say the magic word and things will somehow straighten themselves out at the End of Time. Doesn't it make more sense to believe that God is partly working out the details here and now, through each person who will yield to His influence?"

"I suppose so. And that brings us back to D's question: 'What role does a Personal God play when we're busy here at the office?' GM's answer is that God is working through us to make the world better, in every possible way, no matter how secular. And God is trying to do it through all of us, to whatever extent we'll let it happen."

Savannah is thoughtful a moment. "Even through D?"

I nod. "Through anyone who will respond, regardless of their theology. D thinks she's following an impersonal principle, and what does it matter as long as she responds to the influence? But for those of us who believe, there's the joy of fellowship with Someone who dwells within us and encourages us to risk doing greater things."

"GM promised to give concrete examples of that next week," Savannah says. "I'm ready to hear some practical applications."

"Me too," I tell her.

17 WHERE THE RUBBER MEETS THE ROAD

It's Wednesday night again, but this session is quite different from the others we've attended. The parlor is crowded. A number of former members of the group are here to share their stories.

Vivian starts off. She's 50-ish, and she's spent the past twenty years working in the Consumer Loan Department of a small regional bank.

"Three years ago, we were assigned a young Polish supervisor named Elayna. It was rumored that she was really going to shake things up. The other gals in the office just laughed. They called her 'The Queen' and placed bets on how long it would take to break her down. Lizzie was the most vocal. She told Elayna right to her face, 'I've seen supervisors come and I've seen 'em go, but I'm still here, and I'll still be here when you're gone.'"

"Ouch!" we say.

"Yeah. But Elayna was a tough one. She just smiled right back at her and didn't say a word. She was in no hurry to prove anything. But big changes were coming, and Lizzie didn't stand a chance."

"What kinds of changes?" someone asks.

"Oh," says Vivian, "our department was a mess! I had already come to that conclusion months before Elayna showed up. These sessions here at the Cathedral helped me to see that, as GM will tell you."

"Yes," he says, "you were very much in my prayers throughout that period."

"For years," she tells us, "I started out each workday saying, 'Lord, make me an instrument of your peace.' And then I'd just go about my day the best I could, hoping that the prayer was being answered but never actually checking in—never looking for specific ways to live out that prayer. After I started being part of this discussion group, I became a little more aware of what was happening at the office."

"Give yourself more credit than that," GM urges. "You did a lot of thinking about it."

"Yes," she admits. "I began to see all kinds of problems, but I couldn't come up with any solutions. Sometimes it just made me cry. GM and I had some counseling sessions about it, to no avail. I started looking for job openings in other departments."

"Why don't you tell them what the problem was," GM suggests.

"Well, that was the trouble: it was very hard to sort out what the real problem was. All I knew was that our department was a mess. It was divided into factions, with some people favoring one group and others favoring another, but nobody was actually in charge. Brent was our supervisor, but he had no clout. Lizzie was probably the most powerful person in our department, but that wasn't saying much. Only some people listened to her. Others listened to Ebony.

"But the thing was: we had no procedures. New people weren't trained. Everybody did pretty much whatever they wanted to do, however they felt like doing it. And that depended in large measure on who they accepted advice from when they were new-hires. Some followed Lizzie, some Ebony, others struck out on their own; but there was also a lot of variation even within those three camps. It was a free-for-all.

"Sometimes Brent would step in and say we should do it this or that way—usually because Lizzie got upset that somebody didn't do it *her* way—but he never forced us to change or do things uniformly.

"Then Elayna replaced Brent. She seemed like a smart kid. I prayed and prayed for her to take command of the department. One morning as I was unlocking my desk and turning on my computer, I started to say, 'Lord, make me an instrument of your—" and right then, the most amazing thing happened. God spoke back.

"I didn't hear a voice, but I just had this overwhelming thought: 'Do you really mean that?'

"I was shocked. 'Yes I do, Lord,' I said.

"'You want to be an instrument of my peace?' He asked.

"'Yes, of course,' I told Him.

"'But you're going to sit there and let Elayna do what needs to be done—all alone?'

"I shook my head. 'You know I've been praying for her every day.'

"'And I keep waiting for you to act on that prayer,' He said. 'Why don't you do it now?'

"My heart skipped a beat. 'What do you have in mind?'

"'All these months you've agonized about this department,' He said. 'Now someone's finally come to help. Don't you think you should at least offer your services?'

"I looked at Elayna's office. Her light was on and her door was open. Without another word, I got up and went to see her. It felt like an out-of-body experience. I was so scared!

"'Got a minute?' I asked.

"She said yes and I shut the door. I don't think I even sat down. I just blurted it out: 'Elayna, we need procedures. In writing. We've gotta stop this every-gal-for-herself stuff. It's time we standardized our procedures and put them in an online manual. And then we've got to follow them. Everyone. Without exception.'

"Elayna just sat there smiling at me. Then she said in

her heavy Polish accent, 'I know that, Vivvie. I've known it from Day One. I've just been trying to figure out who's passionate enough to do it.'

"'To do what?'

"She looked at me very seriously. 'To write the manual.'

"'I assumed *you'd* do that,' I said, but she shook her head.

"'I will work very closely with the person who does it. *I'll* decide on the procedures. But I'm not a writer. I make a much better Queen.'

"I hit her with a barrage of objections, but she just sat there smiling at me. Then I said, 'What about Lizzie and Ebony and the others? They'll hate me.'

"'You're right,' she said. 'They will. But they'll get over it.'

"I kept thinking of all the reasons I couldn't do it, then I heard an inner voice—not God's this time, but my own. It said, 'Lord, make me an instrument of your peace.' And that's when I realized I had to do it."

Savannah shakes her head incredulously. "Did you know anything about technical writing? Did you have any experience posting files online?"

"None whatsoever. I was also unprepared to deal with the office politics. But Elayna stood by me 100 percent. And I prayed about everything after that—every detail all through the day.

"Were you asking God to micromanage?" someone quips.

She shrugs. "It wasn't that I wanted or needed God to micromanage me. I just wanted to keep my soul open to that inexhaustible Source. I drew on it all day, in lots and lots of ways.

"That was three years ago. We're an entirely different outfit now. Lizzie and Ebony are still with us. They're productive members of our team. Nobody calls Elayna 'The Queen' anymore, but they do what she asks, because they respect her. And they have a certain amount of respect for me, too. After I finished the online manual, I was given other things to do. I haven't been promoted, but I suppose that'll come, in time.

"I no longer pray to be made an instrument of God's peace, although that desire is the guiding force behind every request I do make. It's just that my prayer life is so rich now—so content-oriented—that I just don't fall back on general prayers like that anymore."

All over the room, people raise questions, and after Vivian has answered a few of them, someone asks, "GM, does it have to be something that dramatic? Does God ever help with small, day-to-day stuff?"

That prompts a number of others to tell their stories.

"It can be something so basic," a thirty-something woman says. "I had a great job with a good company and wonderful people, but I just couldn't keep up. My supervisor and I had numerous talks about it but I always felt like I was playing Catch Up. I'd take work home at night and I'd go into the office on weekends, but I just couldn't seem to get ahead.

"Then I took GM's advice and prayed about it. You'll never guess what the answer was."

We wait, and then she tells us.

"It turns out I just needed to clean my desk."

"Huh?"

"Well, that wasn't the whole thing, but it was the turning point. I'm an extremely neat person. I can't tolerate a messy desk, but when I came into this position, I had to hit the ground running. I was so busy trying to do the job, I never had a chance to get organized. I knew my workspace was a Disaster Area and I hated that, but I also had nowhere to go with the different stacks of paper on my desk.

"This may sound silly, but after praying about it, I asked around and learned we had an extra table that wasn't being used. I put it in the corner of my office and laid out all the papers that had been piled on my desk. Then I got some desk organizers and put them into manageable groups. Once that was done, then I was able to organize my work mentally. It's a simple thing, I realize, but that's what got me back on my feet.

"I should add, though, that my job is inherently open-ended, and that was the second thing my prayer life made me realize. I'll never get caught up. That's the nature of my job. Through prayer, I not only became aware of that fact but also became reconciled to it."

GM gestures to me. "Remember your question about Clifford the Big Red Dog, Dayton?"

I nod.

"God isn't just watching through the window while we work. God is available for a consultation at any time, about any aspect of our jobs."

"But is that the full extent of it?" someone asks. "Or does God actually help us, too?"

A number of people try to answer at once.

A teacher says, "I can only do so much to get a point across in the classroom. Quite often something serendipitous happens that makes it click for a particular student. I have no control over it, but I factor it in whenever I'm planning a lesson."

Someone else says, "I'm responsible for generating reports, and some of the data has to come from people in other departments. I can plead with them to do their part, but I can't make it happen. Occasionally when things seem at a standstill and I can't get the other people to cooperate, I pray about it and we somehow work it out."

"The point here," says GM "is that God is not just a silent observer. Through prayer, we can receive guidance and even intervention at times."

"And sometimes," a young man adds, "God can help you even if you're not any good at praying.

"I sell advertising for a suburban newspaper," he says. "I'm a talker. I'll talk your ear off if you let me. When I started my job, I wasn't making the kind of progress I was expecting, so I prayed and prayed about it, but it didn't seem to help. Of course, when I prayed, I did the same thing: I talked and talked at God.

"Then I visited GM, and he suggested that I stop

talking God's ear off and just listen. I had no idea what he meant.

"I set aside some time in my apartment and I tried it. I honestly did. I just sat there listening. But all I could hear was the sound of TVs and stereos in other apartments. I heard the couple next door yelling at each other. There were dogs barking. I just got more and more frustrated. What was I supposed to be listening for? It seemed like a waste of time.

"The next morning, I drove down to Main Street in the little suburb where I work. I walked up to the first shop, and as I opened the door, I heard a voice."

He turns to Vivian. "*I* actually *did* hear a voice, Vivian, but it wasn't the voice of God. It was the voice of Dr. Grizzled Mane!"

Everybody laughs and looks at GM. He laughs, too.

"The voice said, 'Don't talk. Listen.'

"It was really hard for me, but I did it. I sat down with that merchant and told him I was a salesman for *The Journal*. Then he started in on me, explaining all the reasons why he wasn't interested.

"I resisted the temptation to talk. Instead of arguing with him or giving him my spiel, I asked him questions about himself and his business. To my surprise, it was really interesting. After a while, I thanked him for his time and admitted that I had learned a lot. I gave him my business card and told him I truly believed that *The Journal* was the best investment for his advertising dollar, but I didn't press him.

"Then I just went down the street, meeting the other merchants and showing an interest in their businesses. That was the first step on my way to building their trust. I had no idea at the time, but *that* was the main thing. They needed to trust me first. Once they did, *then* I could give them my spiel."

Then he adds, "Funny story. After I started being the leader on the sales board, my boss used me as an example for the rest of the staff. At one of our team meetings, he said, 'I want everybody to try Jack's technique.' I'm sitting there wondering, 'What's my technique?' Then I realized: 'Ohhh! He wants them to listen to the customer!'"

"Imagine that!" somebody says, and we all laugh.

Others tell their stories. The most unlikely of these is a bill collector.

"I understand why the public thinks we're low-life," he says. "We're not the most sympathetic people around. We're persistent. We won't take No for an answer. We threaten delinquent customers with legal action. When necessary, we foreclose on their homes or repossess their vehicles. All of these things make us look like bad guys.

"Many of my colleagues go even farther. They insult delinquent customers. They yell. They resort to name-calling. And when an otherwise innocent person gets behind in his payments, an experience like that can be terrifying. It can make him bitter for the rest of his life."

A lady near us is looking down at her feet. Her face is flushed, and she's nodding vigorously.

"But I believe that my line of work is needed in this society. When a company delivers goods or services and the customer doesn't pay, that company has a right to payment. The customer received the goods or services and owes that company the money. It's my job to help work that out.

"I started attending these sessions here at the Cathedral a few years ago, and it made me do some constructive thinking about my job."

"I remember that," GM says. "Can you tell us what you learned?"

"Well, as I prayed about it, the first thing I realized was that I needed a wider repertoire. There were lots of different kinds of people out there, and I was using the same general approach with all of them. I began to see that they fell into three broad categories: those who were serious about paying their debt, those who would do so if prodded, and those who had no intention of paying."

"How did those categories help you?"

"They showed me more clearly how to approach people. The first group just needed my support. They had every intention of paying, so I just had to stay out of the way. Anything I could do to make it easier for them, I did. If they didn't have a stamp to mail the payment, I offered to take it electronically. If they needed an extension until next Tuesday, I could wait, because I knew they were serious about paying. Other than that, I just thanked them for their cooperation. There was no need to get ugly, and certainly no point in antagonizing them.

"The second group would pay if prodded. That meant I had to be persistent and no-nonsense, but it wasn't necessary to threaten them or raise my voice. I just had to stay on them and insist that they pay me.

"The third group was my biggest challenge, because these were the people who had no intention of paying. But as I prayed about it, I realized that even this group was made up of different kinds of people. Some would just try to dodge my phone calls, while others would go on the attack. Some would pretend to be friendly and apologetic, but they were lying through their teeth. Every customer was different. That became the funnest part of my job: figuring out who was who and finding innovative ways to get them to pay."

"It sounds like it was a discernment process," GM says.

"It became that, yes. I used to just yell at those kinds of people and tell them I'd see them in court. But once I started praying about it, I began to realize that yelling was counterproductive. In some cases, that was exactly what they wanted me to do. I don't fall for that anymore. I work very closely with God now, as strange as that may sound. I ask Him to help me figure out who I'm dealing with, and if possible, to gain their cooperation. A lot of people won't pay at all, but I've managed to get resolution from some of the most unlikely characters, just by understanding them and making it in their own best interest to pay me."

This prompts an operations manager to tell about his experiences dealing with a variety of union representatives. "I came into my job dead-set against union leaders. I thought they were all a bunch of crooks. But I prayed about it, and I learned to get along with the local representatives. Now we're like a well-oiled machine. When the employees have a problem, their representatives come to me and we work it out. When *I've* got a problem, I go to them and—surprisingly—they work with me. It's all about cooperation."

On and on it goes, throughout the night. Savannah and I are amazed at some of the things people pray about in their jobs. This is what we've been looking for: a lively interaction with God in the midst of our daily activities. Not a regimen of Bible study and prayer only, but of real-life exploration. Not a retreat from the secular world but a deep-dive *into* it—with God.

"It occurs to me," I say, "that *we* determine, to some extent, what God does from 9 to 5."

"Why do you say that?" GM asks.

"Because what God does in our lives depends, in large part, on what we ask for. So we set the limits. And that's why so many Christians haven't discovered God in the work world—because they don't ask for guidance on the job."

"That's an interesting thought," he says. "Our lack of receptivity does set certain limits on what can happen. Bear in mind, though, that God is quite adept at overcoming the obstacles we throw in His way. I myself have been surprised at some of the things I've asked for in prayer. 'Where did that come from?' I've wondered. It was like a sudden stroke of genius that opened up new possibilities. God doesn't just answer our prayers; oftentimes God inspires them, too."

The evening is over too soon. Afterwards, we go around the room meeting people, and we exchange phone numbers and email addresses.

We thank GM for devoting so much of the group's time to answering our question. When we tell him about Simon and the morning commute that started all this, he looks shocked. "He wanted you to answer the question during a single bus ride? It took me three weeks to do it!"

There's such a look of amazement on his face, we have to laugh.

But we're both deep in thought as we leave the parlor and walk down the hallway. Savannah turns to me and points at my forehead, then back at her own. That's one of our secret hand signals.

"I'm thinking about Sammy," I tell her.

"From the bus?" she asks.

"Yes. Tonight we heard the testimonies of a number of people who've experienced God in their day-to-day lives. They didn't have to terrorize us with the threat of impending death or hit us over the head with the scriptures. They just told us how God has been revealed to them in their jobs. It seems to me that that kind of sharing is much more effective than the kind that

Sammy does."

She nods. "Well, I've been thinking about Simon. He said that none of the Christians he's met have been able to tell him how God is relevant to their daily lives. He must not have met any of the Christians who were here tonight!"

"GM never mentioned evangelism," I say, "but it was demonstrated powerfully just now. Can you imagine the effect it would have on our society if people in all walks of life found God from 9 to 5—and then told others about it?"

On our way out, we see the cathedral sanctuary lit up and decide to have a better look. As we cross through an arched doorway into the nave, our faces turn upward. Spanning the length and breadth of the ceiling is a magnificent tiled mosaic.

"Dayton, look!"

It's an artistic representation of our own city, with its signature skyline. Cars and trucks can be seen on the freeways, and pedestrians on the sidewalks. Planes are coming and going from the airport. The city is bristling with activity. Above it, with outstretched arms, is the Risen Christ. The text of John 5:17 surrounds the image:

> *My Father is still working,*
> *and I also am working.*

"I believe that now," she says. "More than ever. Do you?"

I nod. "But what are we going to do about it?"

We say nothing more. We just stand there, gazing into the eyes of Jesus… and thinking.

INDEX

ABOUT THE AUTHOR

Ronald R. Johnson is the author of *Customer Service and the Imitation of Christ*. He has a Ph.D. in Philosophy from Saint Louis University and teaches at Spring Arbor University in Michigan (USA). He also has extensive experience working in customer service call centers, both as a frontline CSR and as a manager. He has published articles in *Religious Studies, Philosophy and Rhetoric, The History of Philosophy Quarterly, Philosophy Now, The Way of St. Francis, and Alive Now*. He has devoted his life to finding points of contact with God in the secular world, and he blogs on that subject at http://rjmythicadventures2.wordpress.com. He lives with his wife Nancy and daughter Emily in Portage, Michigan.

53466555R00111

Made in the USA
Charleston, SC
10 March 2016